William J Fay 4.10
#840

P9-CMS-921

THE END
OF THE
HISTORICAL-
CRITICAL
METHOD

THE END OF THE HISTORICAL- CRITICAL METHOD

Gerhard Maier

**Translated by Edwin W. Leverenz
and Rudolph F. Norden**

Publishing House
St. Louis

Gerhard Maier

"Das Ende der Historisch-Kritischen Methode"
Original publication by Theologischer Verlag Rolf
Brockhaus Wuppertal
© 1974 by Theologischer Verlag Rolf Brockhaus
Wuppertal

Translated by permission of Theologischer Verlag Rolf
Brockhaus Wuppertal
Library of Congress Catalog Card No. 76-56222.
Copyright © 1977 by Concordia Publishing House
for English edition
Manufactured in the United States of America

Library of Congress Cataloging in Publication Data

Maier, Gerhard.
    The end of the historical-critical method.

    Translation of Das Ende der historisch-kritischen
Methode.
    Bibliography: p.
    1. Bible—Criticism, interpretation, etc.—His-
tory. 2. Bible—Evidences, authority, etc. I. Title.
BS500.M2413   220.6'07   76-56222
ISBN 0-570-03752-2

CONTENTS

5

FOREWORD

Historical-critical methodology cannot be claimed as a neutral discipline. It holds sway in "scientific" theology pretty much as evolutionism rules the scientific disciplines. Theories multiply, often with total disdain for the facts, at times even though the facts contradict the conclusions. People finally believe what they want to believe. In the name of scholarship man sets himself up as lord over the Word and the work of God.

The historical-critical approach to the Bible has its history, of course. Johann Salomo Semler (late 18th century) is usually designated as father of the technique which not only handled the Bible as an object for historical scrutiny and criticism, but also as a book little different from and no more holy than any other, and surely not to be equated with the Word of God. Very plainly he was saying that he rejected the divine inspiration of the text. This was but a symptom of his total theological stance, a tip of the iceberg so to speak. His was really a revolt against miracles and the supernatural in general, and against heaven in particular. God's supernatural activity in history simply was not in Semler's "book." Not unexpectedly, under his and others' hand, the Bible text and content suffered deliberate vivisection. The surgery was often quite radical and overt, without benefit of anaesthesia for those directly affected by it in the churches. What had happened to the Word meanwhile? Where to locate the Word of God? Many scholars seemed to be unconcerned, since what they were wrapped up in was such exciting business.

A few of the practitioners of higher criticism eventually realized that, when you destroy the thing you are attempting to dissect, you may be putting yourself out of business. The Bible's central message, they reasoned, must in some way be anchored tightly. There must be a mooring point for Christian truth. This minimal "message" must at all costs survive if the theological task itself is to last.

Gerhard Maier's great contribution is precisely at this point. If scholars themselves determine what that Word or "message" is, then plainly they are responsible for establishing whatever is canonical about the canon. Obviously this can be a very subjective exercise. With each exegete or Bible scholar conceiving it to be his task to locate the "canon in the canon," there can be no guarantee of that message, or the Word. Whether those involved in it knew it or not, and no matter how pious their intent, the fact remains that it was a self-defeating process, doomed to failure. Various theories supplanted each other in succession. Maier shows brilliantly that the so-called scientific pursuit in Biblical criticism fell apart on its own "findings." The historical-critical practitioners had themselves become morticians at the funeral and burial of the Word of God.

When this remarkable little book first came to my attention in the German original, I stated in a review article of it in the *Springfielder* (March 1975):

> If there really were a "canon within the canon," a "Word of God" which had to be separated from the Scriptural text, then the result would be not only a dividing of the Holy Scriptures from the Word of God, but also a setting of Christ Himself apart from the Scriptures (and so also the Holy Spirit) in a way unwelcome to each of them—in fact, one "Christ" from another "Christ." Thus, the whole assault of the historical-critical methodology on the Bible must be seen as an irrational, self-defeating sort of folly that has spelled its own doom. It is simply Docetism *redivivus*—the old heresy according to which Christ did not really come into the flesh, but a mere phantom-Christ was crucified. The only new factor is that this time the target is the Scriptural Word, which gives the appearance of being the Word of God, though it really is not; for what appears to be the Word of God is really only a phantom-Word. The Church must repudiate the new as it did the old Docetism! (p. 296).

If we are to have the Word of God in our day, there can be no divorcing of theology and the preached Word in the churches from the authoritative text of the Bible itself as the Word of God. Divine inspiration is "the true canonization" of the Old and New Testaments, stated Martin Chemnitz in his immortal *Examen Concilii Tridentini.* (See the English translation, *Examination of the Council of Trent*, Concordia Publishing House, 1971, p. 136.) "We have . . . a more sure word of prophecy, whereunto ye do well that ye take heed . . . Scripture" (2 Peter 1:19 f.).

Beyond cavil, therefore, Maier's book fills a real need. It was time that higher criticism be seen for what it is, an uncritical and unjustified denigration of the Biblical text. It had become a godless technique that eroded the Word of God itself. Acting all the while like the dutiful handmaiden of theology, it left the church dangling with the unanswered question of where to find the Word of God if its (higher criticism's) assumptions were accepted as true. Maier reveals the denouement of higher criticism's intrigue by simply showing how one scholar in effect and in fact repudiates the thinking and conclusions of the other, and so on down the line, with the Bible itself, though buffeted in the process, finally coming off unscarred. The careful reader may want to express a stricture here and there; for example, anent the doctrine of the church and chiliasm; ·but these become incidental to what overall is a masterful piece of work that must be gratefully acknowledged as needed by the church in our day.

Eugene F. Klug

I.
THE INNER IMPOSSIBILITY OF THE CONCEPT

1. Introduction

The general acceptance of Semler's basic concept that the Bible must be treated like any other book [1] has plunged theology into an endless chain of perplexities and inner contradictions. This concept, which attempted with increasing satisfaction to show contradictions in the Bible, accomplished its utmost just in this. In its development, what began as a *characteristicum protestanticum* (Protestant characteristic) culminated in a universal Christian sickness. One can hardly express it differently.

All phenomena in this area are especially related to the concept of the historical-critical method. A method which is not only asserted but is used as a scholarly tool—and this has constantly been the practice of theological Christian scholarship—represents a prejudgment in the sense of an a priori decision concerning the outcome. Modern physical research could teach theology in this area how the selection of a method of study can predetermine and prefigure the scope, extent, and type of results. Accordingly, a critical method of Bible interpretation can produce only Bible-critical propositions. This is true even in those instances where the historical-critical method confirms Bible propositions. For the justification and authority of the outcome are still established by the critical scholar himself and, due to the method, cannot come only out of Scripture.

The historical-critical method, in its actual application, has become an impenetrable screen which simply does not allow certain statements anymore, even though they may be proved a thousand times in the experience of believers. This is not evil intent but the helplessness into which a falsely selected method blunders.

To stigmatize with the term "supranatural" or (in the sense of this one method) "unscholarly"[2] will suffice to permit the ostracizing power of the screen to take effect. In that case one just isn't "in" anymore. All the while the historical-critical method has become an instrument in the hands of the exegetes with the help of which they have pushed through a truly dictatorial regime in theology. Dogmatics, the centuries-old queen of theological studies, became a domestic servant who was still permitted to arrange, systematize, preserve, and classify everything, yet who was always required to seek the approval of historical-critical exegesis before she was permitted to make any statements to the outside world. Even the most guarded caution could not protect her from the ridicule of the exegetical Caesars.

Only recently was this development stopped through the encroachment of utopian-Marxist thought into Christian theology, together with its accompanying contempt for the "merely historical" branches of theology. Very suddenly the prevailing exegesis tumbled from its high pedestal and was swept into a corner. It is now even more imperative that exegetes devote more sincere and unbiased attention to their basic concepts and methods.[3]

2. The Nature of the Historical-Critical Method

What does the designation "historical-critical" imply? It does have one element which obviously has justifiable support in historical change and in man's experience of God—the historical. Since this aspect will be discussed at greater length later, it may be passed over here. This, however, may be noted in passing, that the revolutionary impulse of the method was naturally not in the historical, nor was that aspect given primary emphasis. The Reformation movement almost self-evidently brought into prominence the historical aspects of Biblical and church tradition. It would not be difficult, especially in the writings of Luther himself, to find a host of examples of this—from his pronouncements concerning the "moving rain showers" of the Word of God to his opinions on the establishment of the canon. The covenant theology of the Bremen exegete Koch might be cited as another example to show that the consciousness of the historical element remained alive also during the so-called orthodox paralysis. And finally, one may be reminded that Pietism generally meant a reawakening of apocalyptic-eschatological thought. The Pietists enjoyed speaking of the "economies" of the divine history of salvation revealed in the Word of God. They also revived some of the eschatological thoughts of Joachim a Fiore.[4] According to all appearances, a determined use of a purely historical method would not have sparked a revolution in theological thought in the field of exegesis. Rather, it would probably have meant the continuation and perhaps fruitful enrichment of previous work in this area.

It is therefore of decisive significance to recognize that the initial and constantly expanding revolution was associated with the word "critical." The "critical" was the motor and the accelerator of the movement. On it rested the determining accent. In the field of the critical lay the numerous assumptions of the new method—assumptions that were questioned less and less and were often protected simply by the "modern outlook"[5] or, even simpler, by the sentence: "We just can't go back beyond that."[6]

We mention only briefly the developments associated with the beginnings of the historical-critical method.[7] English deism had ceased leaving untouched the assumption of a revelation and the distinctiveness of Christian knowledge of God's dealings. In Matthew Tindal and other representatives deism progressed to the concept that human reason, as a meaningful creation, is the touchstone and yardstick of everything revealed in Scripture. Anything that could not be proved and established by it had to be dismissed. French skepticism took on an even more radical look. Transcendence was finished off in *L'homme machine;* materialism celebrated triumphs. Baron de Holbach and Voltaire aggressively scoffed at Biblical revelation and ridiculed its representatives.[8] In Germany, to be sure, there was more caution. One must remember that during the German Enlightenment the figures of a Herder, a Jung-Stilling, or a Lavater enjoyed general respect and even the admiration of a Goethe. It must also be borne in mind that a contemporary movement during the Enlightenment was Pietism, which had tremendous influence and flourished more than once. But the overwhelming majority of the intellectuals, especially in northern Germany, looked to Reimarus as their spokesman and were jubilant about Lessing's victory over the head pastor of Hamburg, Goeze. The yearning of the time was crystallized in the concept "freedom." For most people of that era this meant freedom also from the divine principles of revelation, interpreted as ecclesiastical morality, and from church authority, which they rightly or wrongly saw as part of the political and secular power structure. Kant's well-known epithet that the Enlightenment dealt with man's emergence from his self-imposed immaturity was in practice interpreted as a battle for freedom against all sinister, oppressing forces, among which the church was included.

Perhaps it would be incorrect to explain the "critical" element of the new theological method only by attributing it to the influence of the spirit of the Enlightenment or to the theological reaction in a defensive battle, or even to both of these. Certainly education, which since the Renaissance was based on Socratic ideals, played an important role. Contrary to the Scriptural viewpoint, Greek-Roman [humanistic] education permitted conscience and will to be guided by knowledge. Closely associated with this was the glorification of the *kalos k'agathos,* of the *anthropos metron hapantoon.*[9] Carrying over such basic principles into theology could only have the result of weakening the *pondus peccati,*[10] especially in regard to the use of human reason. As reasons for the change in theology, in additon to the constantly widening world horizons and the increasing knowledge about other peoples and other religions, one may cite the church's constant loss of power and importance in the daily life of the people, the relativizing striving for tolerance, the noticeable signs of a "people's religion," and so forth. It is, however, not necessary here to present the historical development of the historical-critical method with indisputable evidence for all its aspects. After all, it has been one of its own basic evils to imply that with the historical sequence of certain thoughts everything has been explained and said; this very thing corresponded with Greek-Roman education. Furthermore, we cannot rule out that the development of this theological method was basic to apocalyptic-eschatological points of view. The decisive factor today is that we must take advantage of the opportunity, in a time of breakdown and of greater perspective over against its origin, to develop a new orientation.

The question is: Is this method (historical-*critical*) suitable for use with this subject matter (Bible, revelation)?

As we now turn to this question of the adequacy of the method and its concept, we first need to establish what, after all, the historical-critical method aimed to do. We now attempt to give a sort of cross section of that objective. This cross section reveals an enduring conviction which had its approximate starting point in Semler's sentence: "The root of the evil (in theology) is the interchangeable use of the terms 'Scripture' and 'Word of God.'"[11] Its preliminary goal becomes discernible in Kaesemann's statement that in the New Testament faith and superstition are both in the arena at the same time; he therefore wants to retreat "from the incomprehensible . . . superstition that everywhere in the canon only genuine faith is proclaimed."[12] Biblical criticism therefore followed the positive goal (at least understood as positive by it) to clearly mark on the one hand what was only formally Biblical, specifically the "spurious" faith, and on the other hand the "genuine" faith, specifically to dig out what is binding. We must deny ourselves the fascinating task of presenting the many variants and the often completely dissimilar results of such work.[13] Our attention can be given here only to what is basic.

Some light should now be shed on these basic principles. Again the question arises: What was it that led the individual theologians to their critical point of view and to their daring courage? One cannot help but note that alongside of critical theology—indeed in touch with it and even in opposition to it—runs the line of "Biblicism," "fundamentalism," etc., in similar solidity and constancy. In Germany, to be sure, it is much weaker than, for example, in the Anglo-Saxon areas; for a time it was also "submerged" under the scholarly standard of the so-called "community theology" *(Gemeindetheologie).* One frequently hears[14] that the awakening historical consciousness and the historian's practice of his profession forced that separation. Such an explanation can rightly be doubted. It seems to make things foggy rather than to clear them up. For also the "Biblicists" understood how to work historically, some of them as simply and honestly as the "criticists." Finally and above all, we are by no means in the area of the purely historical, but at best in that of historical *theology,* and the judgment as to what is genuine and what is not genuine faith is simply no longer a historical one.

To be sure, as long as one makes analogous classification a precondition for acceptance, much in the world of the Bible remains without foundation. But how can the *pure* historian without further ado reject something just because it happens only once? What can be experienced and what has analogies can certainly not be declared synonymous. Therefore only the rightly closed realm of biography remains available to us in order finally to answer that question about the root of the critical stance.[15]

3. Objections to the Historical-Critical Method

a) It Is Impossible to Discover the Canon in the Canon

It is evident that the attempt to dig out the Word of God in Scripture, or what is genuine and binding in the Bible, inescapably leads to the obligation of finding "the canon in the canon." If one does not want to give himself up to subjective, arbitrary action, then objective standards, generally convincing, must be established. Protestant theology has used several of these, of which Luther's "what teaches Christ" *(was Christum treibet)* is most widespread and best known. More recent Protestant theologians have moved to the pinpoint of the Pauline-Reformation proclamation of justification (Joest, Kaesemann).[16] Others take recourse to the oldest proclamation *(kerygma)* of the New Testament, and at the same time they add that one cannot exactly grasp this with their methods (Kuemmel, Marxsen);[17] or they pick out a whole block of writings for this purpose (H. Braun).[18] All such attempts thus far undertaken have ended in failure. To be sure, there was a recognized "canon in the canon" for a time in certain theological schools, but no solution has been acceptable to any church or even to a generation. One reason for this was that either the standards were not exact enough or not convincing enough, or the results, in spite of similar-sounding standards, were still too dissimilar. "Their witness did not agree together" (Mark 14:59). The primary reason, however, for the inability to come up with satisfactory answers is the simple fact that the Bible itself gives no key with which to distinguish between the Word of God and Scripture, and along with that, between Christ and Scripture. This implies at the same time that the method and the object of investigation evidently could not be brought into true relation with each other. Obviously the attempt was falsely "constructed."

b) The Bible Does Not Permit Itself to Be Separated into a Divine Scripture and a Human Scripture

We forge ahead to the next point. We cite again an accepted characteristic of the separation within the formal Bible, namely, the previously quoted sentence (from Semler): "Divine truths commend themselves forthwith because they are for the common good."[19] In our context it all depends on what the concept "divine truth" is. Its meaning, of course, derives from the contrast to "human truth," which allegedly makes up the other part of the Bible. It seems to come awfully close to Lessing's "necessary rational truths."[20] Therewith the whole unhappy area of timeless and time-limited truths, of shell and kernel, in the Bible opens itself up. No one has the right to stamp a representative of the historical-critical method as an unrestrained subjectivist. But is this to say that what is here and now perceived to be eternal was likewise perceived as eternal yesterday and must be so perceived tomorrow? Is this "eternal" something other than an important value of the present time? And even if we should stumble upon such "eternal" truths, as Semler and Lessing identified them, how do we make sure they are not merely human voices that sound divine and that ultimately will have absolutely nothing to do with *theo-logein*, with divine revelation? Semler's definition, which associates the divine with the common good, cannot make us more certain. And how often has not the doctrine of justification already been in danger of becoming simply God's yes and nothing more, or a mere "being accepted" and nothing more!

Pragmatically, many different levels within the Bible have been pointed out in this way, both qualitatively and quantitatively. Complications developed out of further historical investigation. While there was much dispute as to what was "primary," the exegetical judgment "secondary,"[21] "a product of the [early Christian] community," meant a devaluation. Theologically, statements that were thus degraded to lower levels lost their canonical authority, as one may gather from Kaesemann's conclusion: "Wherever this doctrine of justification is no longer clearly and centrally expressed, the theological authority of the canon comes to an end for me, for it ceases to be specifically Christian."[22] On the other hand, a commentator, proceeding on his knowledge of congregational and continuing development, could stretch out the same canonical authority to Augustine and Luther, or to the present day, simply because it agreed with basic principles.[23]

Meanwhile we hold to the conclusion that use of the historical-critical method divided the Bible forcibly into two Bibles, one human and one divine. In spite of honest endeavor, as a result of the lack of a "key," agreement was never reached as to what firmly and always would have to be considered a part of "divine truths."

c) Revelation Is More Than Subject Matter

Unwittingly we have already touched upon the third point which must be considered. It concerns the general recourse to criteria of content. Again a continuous line is drawn from Semler's "divine truths," which have been proved to be "for the common good," to Marxsen's determination of canonical legitimacy, which is said to consist in "that they hand down the *matter* . . . the revelation, in such a way that in another setting, at a later time, it is preserved or restored."[24]

We introduce here two recent examples. W. G. Kuemmel, one of the most level-headed historical-critical exegetes, says: "The more a text points to the historical revelation of Christ, and the less it has been changed by thoughts from outside of Christianity or through later Christian questioning, the more surely it must be counted as belonging to the normative canon."[25]

H. Braun, who represents perhaps the broadest progressive wing of Bultmann's students, nevertheless wants to identify an "inner middle" in the New Testament, which appears "in the manner in which man is seen in his situation before God."[26] It need hardly be proved that statements about content are here made into determining characteristics for divine revelation. To be sure, it would be wrong to argue that historical-critical representatives lack every awareness of the person-structure *(Personstruktur)* of revelation.

For the sake of fairness we must also cite Strathmann's

sentence: "The Biblical concept of truth is not doctrinal-juridical, but personal."[27] In a similar way Ebeling has stated that the determining factor is "not a fixed doctrine, not a law, not a book of revelation, but rather the Person of Christ" as "the total concept of that which is to be transmitted."[28] However, when the Person of Jesus is the subject of transmittal of theological endeavor, the person-structure again begins to fade from view. And how difficult it is to overcome the method's necessary tendency can be seen from Kaesemann's attack on Strathmann: "How can a concept of truth be personal? To what extent should not attachment to a person lead to doctrine? . . . What does the statement about the 'form' *(Gestalt)* of Christ . . . say specifically for faith?"[29]

One cannot escape the impression that the Person of Christ here in fact remains a cipher for a complex of theological statements whose emphasis is basically on content. Characteristically, we certainly hear more on the broad lower levels about "the subject matter of Jesus," which it is said must continue, than about the Person of Jesus, transformed historically-critically into many questions marks. Does a method of this type, working with categories of content, grasp the subject correctly? If one confronts himself with the personal structure of the Bible, he will have to answer this question negatively. Such introductory statements as "And God said," "Now the Word of the Lord came," and "Then Jesus answered and said," make up the backbone of Holy Scripture. All through the Old Testament the provisions of the Law are introduced and endorsed with "God said unto Moses," or "Thus saith the Lord." The basis of their validity is therefore not a quality that is positively provable, but a personal will. If St. Paul appeals to a "command of the Lord,"[30] or when Jesus says, "But I say unto you,"[31] the situation is identical. Because the Lord is speaking, the listener is faced with a divine truth which is binding upon him and which man cannot reevaluate. The historical-critical method, on the contrary, begins with subject-matter information about divine truth in order then to conclude: "Thus said the Lord." Accordingly, the historical-critical method is of necessity concerned with differences of content and judgments about facts, whereas the Bible wants to be a witness of personal encounter and the declaration of the divine will. A suitability of method to subject matter is again diminished or destroyed.

d) The Conclusion Is Established Prior to the Interpretation

A fourth point must now be considered. We again take recourse to Kaesemann's sentence in one of his last utterances. He wants to "move away from the incomprehensible . . . superstition that in the canon only genuine faith manifests itself everywhere." In this late study he also strengthens his viewpoint that in Scripture itself the struggle between God and false gods, between Christ and Antichrist, between faith and superstition is brought to a head; and then he continues: "Scripture . . . to which one surrenders . . . uncritically, leads not only to multiplicity of confessions but also to indistinguishability between faith and superstition."[32] For a moment let us assume that this is really the case. In that event how can the exegete—and not only he—ever reach a correct conclusion as to what is genuine faith? After all, was it not claimed that Scripture left without critical exegesis is marked by the "indistinguishability" just described?

Here it is really interesting to hear what objections Kueng, the Roman Catholic, whose ideas otherwise are not too different from Kaesemann's, raises against him. It seems questionable to Kueng "that he (Kaesemann) himself can know where something is not concerned with the Gospel." It cannot be based on the whole New Testament, and also not on the "findings" of the interpreters. Rather, a Protestant pre-understanding or "some final option"[33] is said to be the basis. "Is not this a position in which one can hardly cite reasons that could prevent someone else from hitting upon a *different* option, and on the basis of another . . . pre-understanding exegetically discovering another middle and another Gospel?" In the end "subjective arbitrariness" would prevail.[34]

Such objections must be taken seriously. They reach far beyond a personal discussion and with the concept "canon in the canon" touch upon the entire historical-critical method.[35] Whenever one has, in line with the method's origins, made it his task to bring to an end the "confusion" between Scripture and God's Word, one had to know in advance what God's Word or genuine faith was. For, as we see, the Bible contains no key within itself to distinguish with absolute certainty between a merely formal "human" Bible and a "divine" Bible. But after all, what should we think of a method which has to bring with it such a conclusive judgment and result before it begins to unlock the subject selected for consideration?

e) Deficient Practicability

The following consideration may bear little weight for a theoretician, but it is of utmost importance for a church that by force of necessity is dependent on guidelines. Of concern is the simple fact that the results of the historical-critical method can show only a very narrow practicability. A peculiar tension reigns between, on the one hand, its supposedly radical commitment, its joy in searching out genuine faith, its revolutionary elan (noticeable on university lecture platforms) and, on the other hand, the retriction which has prevailed for 200 years in its application to everyday practice in the church. Even if the so-called "orthodox" people, or "Biblicists," constantly complained about "liberalism" and resisted its pronouncements—unfortunately only the *pronouncements!*—the fact remains that it was not until the years following World War II that Bultmann's demythologizing program[36] achieved considerable effectiveness in breadth and depth.[37]

Several reasons for this can be given. For one thing, up to the present the higher-critical methodizers could not achieve what in the present political sphere is designated as a "base." Why? Because the results were too complicated, too obtuse. In the second place, the opponents, without wasting too much time on details of the method at work, could as practical churchmen often block the occasional pronouncements with the irrefutable argument: "It's different in my Bible."

Most notable, however, is the third reason. The adherents of the higher-critical method restrained themselves when putting their ideas into practice. For this reason one often heard the complaint from a critically aware public that important and interesting insights were being withheld from them. Typical is the remark by Emperor William II, who noted with reproach in regard to a lecture on "Babel and Bible" by Prof. Delitzsch—himself a member of the Kaiser's German-Oriental Association— that he "unfortunately had discovered a public which was still too unknowledgeable and almost unprepared."[38] The Marburg sermons of Bultmann were classified as "pietistic," and although

21

he held the Virgin Birth and the Incarnation of an eternal Being as a "legend," Bultmann with obvious joy and satisfaction sent to Barth[39] a copy of a Christmas sermon he had delivered.[40] Even though St. John's Gospel happened to be first in the firing line of the historical-critical workers and later, because of defective historical dependability, was rejected in many respects, nevertheless even its critics always found this Gospel to have practical value. Most of them did not hesitate to select confirmation verses containing the "I am" words of Jesus—which according to historical-critical judgment Jesus had never said. And what a great role was played by the statements in the First Letter of John that "God is Love," or "there is no fear in love"[41]—hardly damaged by the critical judgment which sought to recognize First John as not authored by the son of Zebedee but rather as a document originating later in a struggle against heretics. Clergymen who on Mondays stood out as determined representatives of the higher-critical method at their church study groups[42] at the same time were proud of the fact that on Sunday they had preached "normal" sermons that were "faithful to the Scriptures." Enough examples. The question must be asked why the historical-critical exegetes themselves observed this reticence in the application of their ideas.

We do not assume that courage to face the consequences was lacking. At fault was, rather, the objective impossibility of taking the few settlings of knowledge that remained in the sieve of critique and that bore the seal of approval and making them the foundation of practical life in the existing church, or for that matter, in any church. Ultimately, this is where remoteness and estrangement between theological scholarship and congregational life has its roots, not in difficulties of communication. They may well remain until we either change the method or come up with new comprehensive principles or new books of faith. But since also the representatives of the higher-critical method want to be *ecclesiastical* scholars, their conclusions' lack of practicability for the church must be interpreted as a serious objection to their method.

f) Critique Is Not the Appropriate Answer to Revelation

We come to the last consideration of this chapter. Let us

assume that the generally accepted canonical Scriptures[43] are really the witness of divine revelation. No exegesis or theology which concerns itself with scholarly objectivity can preclude this possibility, nor has it desired to do so up to the present. Then, however, it is clear to every knowledgeable observer that in this case and for this subject a *critical* method must fail, because it presents an inner impossibility. For the correlative or counterpart to revelation is not critique but obedience; it is not correction—not even on the basis of a partially recognized and applied revelation— but it is a let-me-be-corrected. Like Job, man must here keep silence because God has something to say to him. He who is to be redeemed has about as much right to stand in judgment about redemption as a patient has the right to change the prescription of his physician according to his own whim. Over against revelation the only way of examining or testing is the experiment: "If any man will do His will, he shall know the doctrine, whether it be of God or whether I speak of Myself" (John 7:17). Jesus is here speaking about *doing* God's will, i.e., carrying out His will with body, soul, and spirit. This experiment is called trust or faith in the New Testament. Anyone who wants prior knowledge without such active faith cannot help but go astray.

In this situation some like to cite the *sacrificium intellectus* (sacrifice of the intellect), implying that God does not demand a sacrifice of reason because it is contrary to creation and therefore repulsive to Him. The whole reference to the *sacrificium intellectus*, however, overlooks two things. First of all, no man exists who can play the role of one who is able to give or who can sacrifice of his own accord when his relationship to God is the subject of debate. And second, human reason, like man himself, as a result of sin is *moribundus* (subject to death) and also *morbidus* (diseased).

From this point of view the wrong approach of the higher-critical method again becomes clear. In opposition to Luther's *De servo arbitrio*,[44] this method would take human reason out of the fall into sin and use it critically, i. e., to discriminate and make judgments in matters of revelation. In actual fact this method has thereby already withdrawn reason from claims to revelation. What blindness! It [this method] does not want to admit that every critique, and therefore the critical method in theology, demands a point of view from which classification and coordination follow and from which judgments and evaluations can take place. Since, of course, criticism initially wants to approach the Bible from the outside, its position toward it cannot possibly be found in the Bible even if it has immediately gained a footing there and now takes the latter as a further point of departure.

Accordingly the higher-critical method, as a matter of basic principle, means a procedure according to which the Bible is approached from an extra-Biblical position and with extra-Biblical standards, with the objective of discovering the Word of God in the process. Pascal's great discovery, "The God of Abraham, the God of Isaac, the God of Jacob—not the God of the philosophers," has become lost in the procedure.[45]

Natural theology has to a certain extent gained the victory over the theology of revelation. Accordingly, the demand is made again and again that a theological statement must "verify" itself (prove its truthfulness). Perhaps no phrase or expression is more characteristic of the method than this one. What is meant, of course, is not verification with the will of God revealed in the Scriptures, but the ability to stand or (in practice much more frequently) at least the ability to sneak by before the tribunal of critical reason.

It does not help much to adduce the "Messenger problem" or the Incarnation as an excuse. For it is the Word of God which became flesh, and God has forever bound Himself to the Messenger: "Till heaven and earth pass, one jot or tittle shall in no wise pass from the Law, till all be fulfilled" (Matt. 5:18). It would be inadmissible to explain the "Word become flesh" as the search of God for man and His method of meeting him, and to suggest again two different qualities, as though there were a so-to-speak fallible human incarnation which our critical reason would be able and allowed to sort out, and a divine, true incarnation which permits itself to be authenticated by our critique. As God finally and conclusively "hath . . . spoken unto us by His Son" as incarnation in the narrower and special sense, so in the Old Testament as "God . . . spake . . . unto the fathers by the prophets," i. e., as deliverers of His message, there is also an incarnation in a broader sense (Heb. 1:1-2). The arbitrary attempt to drive a wedge between His messengers and the One who sends the messengers must fail. This would mean nothing else than searching for an "eternal Gospel" behind the accessible Gospel—accessible indeed to scholarly critics but not to the messengers—and finally ending in an interpretation like that of Marcion,[46] which considers itself above the Scriptures and seeks to gain access directly to the unfathomable decrees of God.

4. Summary

We now summarize. The concept and development of the higher-critical method present an inner impossibility to the extent that one holds to the position that the witness of divine revelation is presented in the canonical Scriptures. The method cannot prove a "canon in the canon," nor can it offer any clarity on the subject of a "divine" and a "human" Bible. In its concentration on subject matter, it is not able to grasp the person-structure of the Bible. The method cannot do without preconceived ideas of what "genuine faith" or "the Word of God" is. Because its results are lacking in practicability, this method is unsuitable or at least inadequate in the eyes of the church. But the most important objection is that historical criticism over against a possible divine revelation presents an inconclusive and false counterpart which basically maintains human arbitrariness and its standards in opposition to the demands of revelation. Therefore because this method is not suited to the subject, in fact even opposes its obvious tendency, we must reject it.[47]

The task of the following chapter will be to demonstrate in a practical way, by means of a concrete yet representative example, what has here been presented in its basic principles. This leads us to the practical end of the method.

II.

THE ACTUAL END OF THE HISTORICAL-CRITICAL METHOD

1. Preliminary Remarks

In the year 1970 a book appeared in Germany which deserves not only the widest distribution but also the most detailed attention. It is the volume bearing the title *Das Neue Testament als Kanon* [*The New Testament as Canon*] (Goettingen), in which Ernst Kaesemann compiled essays of 15 authors of the period 1941—70, accompanying them with his own analysis of the problem. The preface of the book states its objective: "Here exegetes will be queried concerning their systematic assumptions and central themes, and systematicians will give answer to the exegetical challenge." Since the relationship to the problem of the canon is clearly stated, and since with the assumptions and central themes the basic principles of methodology are of course touched upon, the book is of unusual importance to the theme of our present volume. What now follows bears this out.

This becomes even clearer from the selection of authors. Only two of the 15 are members of the Roman Catholic Church.[48] Besides, (Protestant) exegetes are in the majority. This is not meant as a reproach; on the contrary, we consider it useful for the definition and grasp of the problem, which after all first made its appearance in Protestant Christendom and was developed primarily through exegesis.

But what demands special consideration is the fact that this collection of essays representing modern exegesis must be viewed against the background of its development covering a period of two centuries. We are dealing here with nothing else than a balance sheet that demands an accounting.[49] Therefore what has resulted from the course of those 200 years has the character of final conclusions and may well require definitive evaluation. Since only representatives of the higher-critical method are here represented, all extraneous distortion is fortunately absent. What we have before us is therefore an authentic self-testimony.

All these facts underline the importance and function of the book. On the other hand, it also affords a legitimate opportunity to point out the procedure and the final result of the higher-critical method.

The following sequence will be followed: We will first examine the exegetes, then the systematicians, and finally the two church historians with their assertions.[50] E. Kaesemann concluded the book with his own analysis, but here his comments will be considered at the end of the exegetes' section, which seems to suit the subject matter better.

2. The Exegetes: The Abortive Search for a Canon in the Canon

We begin with *H. Strathmann.* Sketched very briefly, his position is approximately this: One must "reject primitive Scriptural proof which assumes that it can prove the Christian legitimacy of a dogmatic statement by citing isolated Bible verses." So a standard, a canon for the actual canon, must be found. This is the responsibility of theological research, which enjoys complete freedom in its work. It may therefore not be regulated ecclesiastically or Biblicistically or in any other manner. Strathmann is of the opinion that Luther already sensed the correct standard: "What Luther said in his preface to the Letter of James concerning 'what teaches Christ' *(Christum treibet)* brings the subject matter to the simply appropriate formula with the intuitive certainty of genius." He makes the general deduction in the form of an alternative: "The Biblical concept of truth is not doctrinal-juridical but personal *(persohnhaft).*[51]

Since the above-quoted principle of Luther's has exerted powerful attraction for some centuries and turns up again and again—also in this book—it is necessary here to blend in a little explanation concerning this quotation. In his famous preface to the epistles of James and Jude in the year 1522 Luther not only established "what teaches Christ" as the standard of his estimate of a book of Scripture, but he also attempted to clarify that formula. Whoever attempts to teach Christian people must accordingly be mindful "of the suffering, the resurrection, and the Spirit of Christ."[52] Because Luther did not find such thoughts in the Letter of James, he does not consider it to have been authored by an apostle and does not want to have it included "in the number of genuine chief books."[53] He even expresses a definite conjecture about its nonapostolic authorship.[54]

Now it is crucial to note the context in which these statements of Luther's must be viewed, and the scope he himself attaches to them. To begin with, one notes in him a certain self-critical limitation and the realization that he was here making an altogether subjective judgment. Thus he says concerning the Letter of James that he wants to "restrain no one from placing or exalting it as he may desire." Since in addition to the Letter of James also the Book of Revelation (among others) was relegated to the Appendix of his New Testament of 1522, we may also quote his remark in connection with the latter: "No one should be obligated to accept my thought or judgment."[55] It is therefore obvious that Luther did not undertake to make the methodically absolute determination which we find in theology since the Enlightenment.

One must, then, constantly be aware of the context as well as the multi-stratification of Luther's theology, in which, of course, the above statements concerning James have their origin. We may remind ourselves of the *est* [is] on the pulpit of the Marburg church with which Luther, clinging to the words of Scripture, obstinately defended substance versus significance[56] in the battle with Zwingli on Holy Communion. Ten years later he wrote in the preface to the Bible: "We must let the prophets and apostles sit at the desk and we, seated at their feet, must listen to what they say, and not say what they must listen to."[57] Without doubt this comment pertains to the entire canonical New Testament as it has been handed down to us, and therewith it proves again that his "what teaches Christ" formula expresses *his* appraisal of the various writings [books of the Bible] and presents *for him* somewhat of a principle of order in the total theological view; but it does not offer a methodological basis in the sense of Semler's separation of Scripture from the Word of God. For the line to a doctrine of verbal inspiration for the entire Bible in accord with the ensuing orthodoxy may be drawn at least as easily as the line to modern higher-critical exegesis.

This becomes even clearer if we now take into account the specific traditional-historical relationship. Luther made more positive judgments on the Letter of James than did the church tradition which was his authoritative standard. Conscious of making judgments in opposition to "the ancients," he writes in his preface of 1522: "I praise the Epistle of St. James and consider it good."[58] The reason for placing it into the Appendix has little to do with his own considerations and certainly has nothing to do with modern criticism of the canon. It is chiefly that "these four (besides James also Jude, Hebrews, and the Book of Revelation)...were in olden times regarded differently,"[59] and Luther in his treatment of the so-called antilegomena[60] wanted to follow as closely as possible the earliest church, which in the understanding of the Reformation was "purer." Apropos of all this, it should not be denied that modern theological criticism did find a starting point in Luther. But it was no more than a starting point. His tendency was in a different direction. So whatever higher criticism may actually carry out with the "what teaches Christ" formula, which has become the key of the critical method, must now be shown in the following modern discussion.

Let us return to Strathmann. It is obvious that for him there is a contrast between "primitive Scriptural proof" and "Christian legitimacy." We see in this the continuation of Semler's separation of "Scripture" and "Word of God." And just for this reason he occupies himself with the canon in the canon—a canon which alone is the Word of God in a material and obligating sense and which presents the sought-for "legitimacy." Among other reasons, such a continuing activity is of interest because Strathmann is looked upon as being in every way moderate and rather conservative in his theology. One can therefore observe how broadly the systematic and methodological presuppositions of the earliest critics have propagated themselves over this period of 200 years.

Next we encounter the contrasting terms "doctrinal-juridical" and "personal" *(personhaft),* with whose help Strathmann attempts to clarify the concept of Biblical truth. Above we had occasion to glimpse as a positive step this clinging to a person-structure in revelation. However, now the question must be asked whether the above contrasting terms really can bring clarification. Naturally, the church of the Reformation, ever since the bonfire in which Luther burned the papal bull and the papal law books, has had little predilection for the juridical. However, as we know, the juridical in the form of a forensic[61] version of the doctrine of justification plays no small role in the New Testament. Some time ago Kaesemann published a noteworthy article on propositions of church law in the New Testament.[62] A legal element was and still is indispensable in the life and structure of the congregation. But much more basic is the statement that the thought cluster of the Messianic Torah[63] or "the law of Christ" or the commandment of Christ[64] exhibits legal elements, that therefore revelation and moral instruction essentially and necessarily belong together. That the Revelator points the way to deliverance is a partial aspect of the claim according to which He (Jesus) Himself is the Way and the Truth (John 14:6). This appears emphatically also in the New Testament statement that Jesus is at the same time the Judge.[65] It is therefore impossible to sever "juridical" from "personal" truth or perhaps even to place them in oppositon to each other.

This, similarly, is true of the concept "doctrinal," which after all has a genuine root in the *doctrina*, or the *didache*,[66] of the New Testament. "He went about preaching and teaching," "He taught and healed," "He taught them all"—in such expressions the evangelists again and again summarize the activity of Jesus. The mission command, " . . . teaching them to observe all things whatsoever I have commanded you" (Matt. 28:19-20) spread the teachings of Jesus abroad to all nations. "Teaching" is one of the primary words in the Acts of the Apostles; it is the subject of Pauline and Johannine admonition—to say nothing of the pastoral letters.[67] In short, revelation and handing down what has been revealed occur extensively in the form of the *didache*, the *doctrina*. It is therefore an imperative conclusion that the contrast "doctrinal-juridical" and "personal" may well be inappropriate for defining a usable canon in the canon.[68]

But now, in the same frame of reference, what about the formula "what teaches Christ," which Strathmann entertains? Luther had attempted to clarify it with three subject areas: the Cross, the Resurrection, and Pentecost. Unfortunately

Strathmann is not able to clarify it further. It would, however, be wrong to reproach him for this. The reproach, rather, must be directed against the formula itself, the moment it is made a tool of the historical-critical method. Justifiably Kaesemann asks the question: "What, precisely, does talking about the 'form' *(Gestalt)* of Christ signify for faith?"[69] The primary flaw of the formula is its lack of precision.

The second primary error was that the "what teaches Christ" formula broke out of the structure of Lutheran theology and in the hands of methodological criticism became a "material principle of selection," as Kueng expresses it.[70] Under the guise of being Christologically centered and true to the Reformation, it makes it possible to justify virtually any critical selection in the canon as we have it. In practice, every original researcher comes up with a different application of the formula. The example of the Letter of James offers a good case in point to clarify this. If one is to begin with Luther's interpretation that this book "makes God's law the main thrust,"[71] then one may ask whether it does not *thereby* point to the need for Christ and therefore teach Christ. St. Paul sees the rightful meaning of the Law in that it is a taskmaster to bring one to Christ (Gal. 3:24; cf. Rom. 7 and 11:32). And does not the Revelation of St. John proclaim the same thing? Which Scripture in the Old or in the New Testament drives one *away* from Christ? Do not all Scriptures serve to drive [the sinner] *to* Him? To be sure, the facts of the case become ponderous when every scholar insists on his own interpretation of "teaching Christ" as the right one. The mere fact that this is possible makes the formula appear to be much too simple and totally useless. Strangely enough, by the way, the formula remained untouched by every change in the picture of the historical Jesus, which ever since Luther has undergone constant change and still continues to do so today.

One will have to conclude from all this that Strathmann cannot convincingly demonstrate a canon in the canon. A solution for the "lingering illness of Protestant theology" which he deplored and which he saw "in the obscurity of its relationship . . . to the Biblical canon"[72] has not been found.

The next essay is by *W. G. Kuemmel.* The author is one of the old masters of the historical-critical method in Germany who, however, is distinguished from more radical proponents by his well-balanced approach and the broad traditional subjects he entertains. For him, too, there is "no question . . . that Luther's principle is entirely correct and that 'whatever preaches and teaches Christ' is canonical." Kuemmel undertakes a practical application of this principle. A part of the New Testament must "the more surely be counted as part of the normative canon . . . the more unequivocally the text points to the historical revelation of Christ and the less it has been changed by non-Christian thoughts or later Christian inquiry."

How can it be established that a text lies so near to the original source? Kuemmel names a stratum for the New Testament which has the advantage of being the most original and can serve as a standard for other texts. To this belong the oldest form of the synoptic tradition, the oldest proclamation *(kerygma)* of the original church, and the theology of Paul. Kuemmel knows full well that the texts can again and again be differently classified and evaluated, according to the viewpoint and development of the critical historian as well as in keeping with the progress of theological research. He writes: "The limit of the New Testament (normative) canon therefore . . . must be determined anew again and again." He is of the opinion that the need for this is God-given, and he sees in the "uncertainty of the limit of the New Testament canon a reference to the incarnation of the Logos."[73]

There is no doubt that Kuemmel succeeded in presenting his systematic and methodological foundations more perspicuously and clearly than we found them in Strathmann. The sharper restatement is now also of help in their critical evaluation. One immediately takes note of the unquestioning attitude with which he proceeds *methodologically* from the duty and necessity of finding a canon in the canon—Kuemmel calls it a "normative" canon. One of the most moving things about the entire volume is that none of the Protestant exegetes or systematicians expresses—either basically or even partially—an uneasiness about Semler's fateful separation of "Scripture" and "Word of God" that might lead to overcoming it. A second characteristic: Kuemmel, with an attitude that takes everything for granted, combines Luther's famous formula [74] with the results of historical research concerning the age, that is, the appropriateness, of a specific text. "What teaches Christ" is what "traditio-historically" is the oldest.

Here, however, uncertainties multiply. There is, first of all, no agreement concerning the oldest form of the synoptic tradition or of the kerygmatic proclamation of the early church—the problem of the "Son of Man" tradition might be an example.[75] Therefore the questions: What did Paul really write in the New Testament? What is essential for a "theology of Paul"? Questions and yet more questions! Every uncertainty must immediately affect the normative canon.

The same thing applies to other texts which, of course, must be brought into a relationship with that oldest level about which hardly any two researchers agree. With that a certain backlash effect occurs. The question which at first is simply historical: how old a text is or who authored it, becomes a burden to the historian, for it automatically becomes a question of evaluating it systematically and theologically. What German research has experienced and suffered with its "form criticism" *(Formgeschichte)*[76] is an example of this.

Out of the above-mentioned second characteristic follows a third: Whatever is "canon in the canon" becomes for Kuemmel and the others who have similar interpretations the exclusive guideline for the historical-critical exegetes. The systematician becomes dependent on their conclusions and decisions. Even worse is that what is "normative" remains obscure for the layman—a pernicious consequence for a "Bible church."

Kuemmel, of course, is certainly not blind to this problem. He justifies it with a reference to the incarnation of the Logos (John 1:14). But does the Incarnation denote the untrustworthiness and uncertainty of revelation? Could one, therefore, speak only of a "that" of revelation, but not of a "what"? Would the Revelator, or His Spirit, who "will guide . . . into all truth" (John 16:13) leave us in the agonizing uncertainty as to what really is normative? Speaking historically, could we imagine that the disciples of Jesus remained in the dark as to what Jesus said—or whether He said it—or what He, with the full authority of His heavenly Father, decided?[77] These would be truly nonsensical conclusions. One should rather question the method which leads to such results.

In any event, it must be recognized that ultimately also Kuemmel no doubt distinguishes between a normative and a factual [78] canon but cannot point the way to a normative canon that is evident or even one capable of being delimited.

We will now query *H. Braun.* As in the case of the previous authors, Braun occupies a certain representative position, i. e., he embodies a very consistent and radical direction of the Bultmann school. Soberingly he summarizes his exegetical findings in this manner: "The New Testament . . . in its most central points has neither a unified report in regard to actual events nor a unified doctrine in regard to the articles of faith." Nevertheless, he speaks of an "inner middle" in the New Testament "out of which, even if not in its entirety, at least essential parts can be comprehended." This "middle," however, can no longer be specified with a Christological formula but is determined anthropologically.[79] Braun sees it "in the manner in which man is seen in his situation before God." "The man who is radically challenged and questioned as the one radically arrested in the Jesus event . . . that is . . . the canon in the canon." The "three big pillars,"[80] Jesus, Paul, John, are the ones who contain such a "middle" and who have normative significance.

One may say that here the "what concerns itself with Christ" formula is superseded by another: "what concerns itself with *me.*" Man as canon in the canon: This has the appeal of a Christianized *anthropon metron hapantoon.*[81] To be sure, several safeguards have been built in to keep it from becoming a shallow humanism. The picturization "before God," for example, can certainly have the character of revelation. Braun would attribute the latter— however understood—also to the "Jesus-event." Nevertheless, the element of revelation is pushed out a bit further than with Kuemmel. This comes about, if for no other reason, because outside of the "three big pillars" the New Testament as normative is not allowed to get a hearing. To be sure, it is not completely to the point when Kaesemann directs the reproach specifically at Braun that he narrows the New Testament down to literary composites and wins his "middle" by a process of reduction.[82] After all, Kuemmel also has his literary composites, such as the "oldest synoptic tradition," which he uses to set the limits of the normative canon. Nevertheless, this procedure of reduction has progressed further with Braun.

Further, one would have to know what the "Jesus-event" really is. Especially here, as is well known, there is no unity among historical-critical exegetes. As Braun himself confirms, no more than a subjective idea has as yet been established because unity of report as well as doctrinal unity are lacking in the New Testament "in the most central elements."

In the end, one has difficulty avoiding the impression that for Braun the assumptions of the historical-critical method—founded on human arbitrariness—logically lead to this, that man himself appears as the norm in the real canon. Man, who began critically to analyze revelation and to discover for himself what is normative, found at the end of the road: himself. Although many of Braun's colleagues who joined him under similar conditions kept their distance from his radicalism,[83] his fearless consistency reveals what inevitably lies at the end of the method's downward road.

Again we hold to the sober conclusion that also Braun in his search for a canon in the canon is neither able to delimit one adequately nor to establish one on a ground other than his own subjective opinion. This is serious in view of the many inconsistencies and contradictions he claims to have found in the canon delivered to us.

W. Marxsen represents the next and presently youngest generation. If the impression is not deceiving, a sheer technical sobriety here manifests itself. Over against the ideological agitation of prior theological conflicts his is a cool type of skepticism which attempts professionally to put the usable remnants into good order. Symptomatic is the popular concept of "subject matter" which now is the object of attention. According to Marxsen, everything must be examined by the "apostolic, irreducible original proclamation." The Christian legitimacy of all other statements, then, is rooted "in this, that they so repeat the subject matter . . . the revelation, that in another setting, at a later time, the subject matter is preserved or restored." So there now enters an element of time which is in principle completely open to the future as to what can claim canonical validity. For when the just-mentioned assumption has been realized, then the sermons of Augustine, Luther, or of the present are just as legitimately and normatively canonical. "Here there exist no differences of canonical quality." Now everything is based on the "apostolic, irreducible original proclamation." Regarding this, unfortunately, Marxsen has to conclude that it "cannot be worked out exactly from the New Testament texts."[84]

So Marxsen wants to proceed purely historically. What is really canonical is arrived at by means of a historical-critical process of reduction. The similarity to H. Braun and W. G. Kuemmel is clear. It becomes more and more evident that Semler's intention of separating "Scripture" and "Word of God" cannot be achieved at all without literary processes of reduction.

However, such a procedure, to the degree that it pertains to a theological subject, is impossible without theological presuppositions. For this reason alone the results will differ again and again. In Germany, for example, the rule was applied that one can safely attribute to Jesus only what cannot be derived from Judaism, from Hellenism, or from the early Christian congregation *(Urgemeinde)*.[85] In opposition to this, the New Testament makes the assertion that in Jesus is fullfilled what the Old Testament had prophesied. It would be misleading *not* to look for Jewish elements in connection with Jesus.[86] On the other hand, it would be just as misleading to expect to find *everything* Jewish about Him. But who should now give information about the truth—except the New Testament?

This example may suffice to indicate the difficulties confronted by the confining processes that have as their aim to ascertain what is irreducible. Marxsen openly admits that the latter "cannot be worked out exactly from the New Testament texts."

In this connection we want to mention two more observations. While Marxsen clings to the concept of "revelation," he defines it primarily with the concept of "subject matter." In the light of the role Jesus fills as the Revelator, or that which the proclaimed Christ fills in the New Testament, all the objections might here be repeated that we in a general way noted earlier under the subject of the "person-structure of revelation." Further, if the legitimacy and binding canonical quality of later statements are dependent on the fact "that in another setting, at a later time, the subject matter is preserved or restored," then a program for all possible "modern" renderings has here been drawn up. On the other hand, however, subjectivity is in no way prevented from saying what it considers correct according to its concept of the setting or the time. The question of what, where, and why something is correct and the uncertainty about true "canonical quality" constitute a conflict from which we shall never be able to emerge. Thus what was begun in historically cool objectivity again culminates in what is incomprehensively subjective.

What was valid above must also be held against Marxsen. In pursuit of the higher-critical method, he is looking for the canon in the actual canon at hand—and beyond this in the entire Christian proclamation—but he just cannot work it out exactly in the New Testament, nor can he free it from the subjective basis to which he is committed.

Now we are anxious to know what *E. Kaesemann* has to say about all this. As editor of the book, he not only includes his earlier essay "Does the New Testament Canon Establish the Unity of the Church?"[87] but in his conclusion he also appends a penetrating analysis which enters into all the comments here presented and evaluates their importance in a critical summary. His factual legitimation of these is without doubt acceptable. We may therefore be permitted to present his position in somewhat greater detail. The starting point of his thinking may be seen in the claim "that historically Yahweh exists only in the struggle with Baal, Jacob exists only in connection with and opposition to Esau," that therefore in the Scriptures faith and superstition are in the arena at the same time.[88] Thereby Scripture is a true mirror of the history-fulfilling struggle between God and idol, Christ and Antichrist, faith and superstition. When we are occupying ourselves with the formal (factual) canon, we step onto a battlefield which demands our research and decision.

For Kaesemann it is an "incomprehensible superstition" to imply that "in the canon only genuine faith manifests itself everywhere."[89] Logically it then becomes an indispensable theological responsibility to carry out a "testing of the spirits" in Scripture and, by means of a trustworthy canon in the canon, to present the "genuine faith" of which we can be certain that here things are said with divine authority. To the critic of this undertaking Kaesemann replies: "The Scripture which one gives over to itself and to which one . . . gives himself up uncritically without the 'principal key' leads not only to a multiplicity of confessions but also to the inability to distinguish between faith and superstition, the Father of Jesus Christ and the idol."[90]

To the essay theme which he himself selected, "Does the New Testament Canon Establish the Unity of the Church?" he not only continues to reply with his famous "No," but he intensifies it while now explaining: "It (the formal canon) establishes also a variety of Christologies which are in part incompatible," yes, "the canon as such also legitimates more or less all sects and false doctrines."[91]

Kaesemann implies that all of this, especially the canon in the canon, can be sufficiently and precisely shown by means of exegesis.

What, then, is that canon in the canon? Kaesemann emphasizes in the first place that no attempt is here made to exclude certain parts of Scripture, as was the case in extreme form with H. Braun, but the concern is with setting a standard for interpretation.[92] This standard he then finds in the justification of the ungodly. Thereby he consciously links up with the Lutheran tradition. He is convinced that in this manner he has clearly and adequately determined "what teaches Christ." But how can, or rather must, historical-critical exegesis stress just this as the center of Scripture and the canon in the canon? He answers: "Because in it (i. e., the justification of the ungodly) the message and words of Jesus stand out as message and work of the Crucified, and His glory and dominion stand out unmistakably from all other religious statements."[93]

The distinctiveness of the argumentation is expressed, above all, in the concept "unmistakably." It is very clear that this exegesis is working toward a subtraction procedure according to which only that can dependably be attributed to Jesus which cannot be explained from any other source. Finally, the following sentences serve as somewhat of a summary: "When this justification no longer gets a hearing clearly and centrally, then for me the theological authority of the canon ends, because it ceases to be specifically Christian. . . . To this extent I do indeed maintain a 'canon in the canon' and at least in principle define its boundaries precisely. To be sure, these become unclear in practice and detail and must ever and again be scrutinized and marked out anew."[94]

We must pause. If one takes an overview of these presentations which focus on the greater part and the most important elements prevailing in current theological discussion, then one runs into a certain assumption which no longer is questioned by Kaesemann. Strangely enough, this assumption is contained in an analogy. *Because* in history God exists only in opposition to idols, and Christ exists only in the struggle with Antichrist, *therefore* both idol and Antichrist must surreptitiously have entered the Scriptures. It should be well noted that we are not dealing with passages in which the Scriptures, so to speak, permit Satan to have his say, but with the message of the various Biblical books, which these books trace back to divine inspiration.

But with this assertion of an analogy Kaesemann runs into a contradiction with the Biblical ephapax, *the "once for all"* [cf. Heb. 7:27; 9:12; 10:10] *of the redemption accomplished through Christ.* Even without regard to the Biblical "once for all" principle, it would logically have to appear doubtful, in the case of a really divine intervention in the course of history, to forcibly prescribe an analogy for God's authorized testimony. Divine intervention in every form of incarnation will lack every analogy to a this-worldly event, and a Scripture brought into being by God's Spirit as witness to it cannot predeterminately be captured in a law of analogy.

Now concerning the justification of the ungodly, every theologian steeped in the Reformation, or in the Bible generally, will immediately give an affirmative answer to its outstanding, its irreplaceable significance. The objections arise where one sees a "qualifying and determining criterion" in the message of justification, or even equates it with what is "specifically Christian."[95] With that it becomes an instrument of minimizing or setting aside other statements of Scripture.

What had to be brought to light as Scriptural truth in the discussion with false teaching on faith and life in a papal church now makes its appearance with the tyrannical deportment of an absolute ruler. This is all the more serious when, as is usual in historical-critical exegesis, the guidelines become unclear and for all practical purposes cannot be firmed up.

Going back to the heart of the matter, we ask: Can one really encompass the redemptive work of Christ adequately in the "justification of the ungodly"? Does not the New Testament concept of *soteria* (salvation), of *sozein* (saving), go further, inasmuch as therein sanctification and healing, yes, the entire eschatological *doxa* (splendor) of God and the Christian are included?[96] One of the most important objections from the exegetical inventory against Kaesemann's concept rests on the fact that with justification the explanatory and speaking aspect of divine action improperly receives primary importance ahead of God's creating and renewing activity. For Kaesemann the *pharmakon athanasias*[97] of the ancient Greek church would have to be an abomination. In spite of that, this key concept has taken up the eschatological elements of the New Testament far better than, for example, focusing on justification as the "determining criterion." Unavoidably Kaesemann comes into tension with what is eschatological and apocalyptic, which he elsewhere defines as "the mother of all Christian theology."[98] One could here mention still other key words which are not necessarily given proper meaning by the doctrine of justification, as for example the atonement (Eph. 1:7) or the new creation (2 Cor. 5:17; Rev. 21:5).

In short, whoever makes justification of the ungodly his focal point on which all theology should be based, and stamps just this as the "specifically Christian," banishes important lines and basic thoughts of Scripture into powerless darkness. By isolating the message of justification, one ultimately robs even it of its function and force. The point is approached where the determining characteristic turns into the "material principle of selection,"[99] to which Kueng objected. Finally and in conclusion, it simply cannot be overlooked that no exegesis can, *coercively* and without revealing prejudice, produce a canon in the canon as a qualifying and determining standard. It is just for this reason that the keys in the history of interpretation break apart. None of these keys is able to put a stop to the misuse of Scripture; rather, every one of them is the gateway to misleading areas. It is becoming more and more evident that the higher-critical method denotes a Babylonian captivity that hands the exegete over to a harmful degree of subjectivity.

Thus, after our examination of the exegetes has demonstrated that none of them was able to delimit or even to discover a convincing canon in the canon, we now take a look at the answers which the systematicians find to the exegetical challenge we have described.

3. The Systematicians: Disagreement and Retreat to Spiritual Experience

Hermann Diem answers in a twofold manner. He admits that a unity of the canon cannot be claimed historically-exegetically. He rejects an attempt at harmonization according to the concordance method. On the other hand, he also refuses to let the exegetes force just any "canon in the canon" upon him. "There is no permanently valid standard for establishing a canon in the canon, even if the viewpoint were 'what teaches Christ.'" He states this refusal out of concern that Scripture might lose the freedom to speak for itself. To be sure, the expositor uses standards, but these are dependent on historical situations and renew themselves again and again when we hear [Scripture]. Only in this way do we ourselves remain free "to hear the entire Scripture, even in those passages which are perhaps still dark for us." Self-evidently thereby a breach is made over against the historical-critical findings, according to which this Scripture possesses no unity. Diem bridges this gap with the help of a dogmatic construction. His helping construction, to begin with, is supported by the "witness of the church." Accordingly "the action of Christ is to be applied to us in its entire scope and fullness, as well as in the total humanness of its proclamation on the basis of the entire Scripture." Basic to this is a second foundation. It consists of the "self-evidence" [100] of Scripture "in the event of its being proclaimed." [101] Also here the thought is of the entire Scripture.

As much as one understands Diem's concern for the freedom of Scripture, so little, nevertheless, does the construction he erects to save it have supporting power. It really represents nothing more than the assertion that the self-evidence of Scripture and the witness of the church associated with it proceed from the possible unity of the Scriptures—which, of course, was denied by the historical-critical exegesis which Diem had recognized! Yes, Diem even denies the possibility of establishing a valid canon in the canon. So this means that the legitimate proclamation brings the opposite of the exegesis. [102]

This is a perplexing result. It pushes us unavoidably into the question: Did systematics here not understand the challenge; or, if the witness of the church is to be validated, is this not the responsibility of exegesis?

Also *Ratschow* grants the witness of the church a decisive position. According to him, there are three elements that establish the canon: "a contingent, complex variety of human testimony, a spiritual experience in the practice of divine worship in the church, and an ecclesiastical decision on this basis."[103] Here it is clear that the "decision" is the big thing, which essentially is based on the spiritual experience of the church and which, in turn, is thought of as a collective whole coming out of the contingent variety of the Biblical testimonies. A further common front with Diem shows up where Ratschow denies a canon in the canon. If one is to treat seriously the thought of the contingency of the real canon, proved in church history, then one may no longer ask the question concerning the "inner reasons" for its origin. It is said that the canon necessarily bears the characteristics of space-time contingency, since this contingency is characteristic also of revelation. So it must be sustained and may not be overplayed by means of a canon in the canon. Ratschow objects especially to the formula "what teaches Christ," saying it does not permit its content to be expanded sufficiently in order to serve as a dependable standard.[104]

Again we sense also in Ratschow the disinclination of the systematician to set up a determining characteristic in the form of a specific, normative canon alongside the factual canon. A convincing disagreement with historical-critical exegesis, however, is lacking. When the systematician rescues himself by referring to the testimony or the experience of the church, he awakens at least the impression that theology as scientific exegesis and congregation as embodied spiritual experience no longer correspond and meaningfully relate to each other.

W. Joest has to a much greater degree stayed in close touch with historical-critical exegesis, and he tries to take up its conclusions and integrate them. From it he takes over the thesis that there are essential differences in the New Testament. At the same time, however, he takes into account the "spiritual experience of the church." How can these two be combined? Joest includes the differences under divine providence. On the one hand, it is true that "in the establishment of the canon there occurs a special gift of God to the church." On the other hand, he ascribes already to the New Testament a "darkening of the witness to Christ . . . which neither for us nor ever for other times in the church is a tool God uses in His activity of effecting His self-disclosure in Christ through Scripture." [105] It must now logically follow—differing from Diem and Ratschow—that within the New Testament the canon in the canon must be lifted out by means of critical discrimination. The freedom to do this is found in the fact that we believe the Biblical witness, not because of formal reasons but because it was the instrument for encounter with Christ. [106] Thus since we found Christ, we can examine the instrument and establish its usefulness and capacity to do the job.

How does Joest establish the normative canon? He, too, draws on the "what teaches Christ" formula: "The sentence that 'that is canonical which teaches Christ' must be affirmed." For him this means "proclaiming Christ . . . as the basis and bearer of justification by grace." Here the systematician finds himself in line with the exegete Kaesemann: "We hold the content of the Pauline-Reformation proclamation of justification to be the real central interpretation of the Word God has spoken in Jesus Christ to us in our situation." [107]

It seems important to direct attention to one point in which Joest, in spite of other deviations, agrees with Diem and Ratschow. This is the assumption of the accuracy of the historical-critical exegesis. It is not questioned. Further, for all three a spiritual experience with Scripture is undeniably present, and it represents a *uniform* Scriptural experience. Behind this, however, questions and questionable statements begin to arise. For example, what is Joest's source for the statement that certain parts of the New Testament never become an instrument of God "at other times in the church"? How then does divine Providence give us the impression that Christ is here speaking through the Scripture that testifies of Him? Does not this become dangerous for someone who has not mastered critical inquiry? Why does the encounter with Christ come into being just in this way? Or do these encounters, as far as Scripture is concerned, permit of many explanations? Finally one is moved to ask: Why is just the "Pauline-Reformation proclamation of justification" the central, therefore the standard and, let us say, the normative interpretation for us in our situation? Joest can substantiate this no more convincingly than Kaesemann. Here also the systematician, at the hand of the historical-critical exegete, falls into a subjectivity which hardly still knows how to make itself understood to others and also falls into a constantly increasing tension over against the spiritual experience of the congregation.

Carefully but unmistakably *Ebeling* likewise makes spiritual experience his starting point. The establishing of canonical quality is, as far as he is concerned, a statement of confession which is finally based on the *testimonium Spiritus Sancti internum* (inner witness of the Holy Spirit). He goes a step further. He sees unity of experience and unity of Scripture inseparably joined together: "Whether its validity as canon has meaning depends on the unity of Scripture." [108] Understandably, from there he rejects a canon in the canon that one could affirm at best only "with the appearance of arbitrariness." Nevertheless for him a dissociation from historical-critical exegesis never comes into consideration; its basic tenets remain for him "outside the area of discussion." [109] Because of this there is a remarkable brokenness in the development of his thought, while results are peculiarly left dangling in the air.

Ebeling implies that just this variety and contradictoriness in the traditions of Biblical proclamation leads to the one *traditum tradendum* (tradition that is to be handed on): "Not an established doctrine, not a law, not a book of revelation, but rather the Person of Jesus Himself...as the authorization of the Gospel." [110] This means nothing else than that the unity of Scripture lies not within itself but outside of itself, in a factor which he describes as "the Person of Jesus . . . as the authorization of the Gospel." The result of this must be that the content of the proclamation remains basically open. What the right hand has just imparted with the concept of the "Person of Jesus" in personal language and category, the left hand, to a certain extent, immediately takes away as it steers us over to the subject matter of the "authorization of the Gospel."

Moreover, since we can learn to know the Person unequivocally only out of the Scriptures of which Ebeling says that they contradict themselves, the question arises: Which Jesus is the one who saves? Somewhat concerned, the reader strikes the balance that also here subjectivity offers the final answer and that the systematician, caught in the tension between spiritual experience of the Scriptures and their historical-critical treatment, does not know how to give a convincing solution.

We have placed the Tuebingen Roman Catholic systematician *Hans Kueng* at the end of our section on the essays of the systematicians. He must certainly be counted as representative of a movement which clings to being Catholic in a good sense but seeks as far as possible to take up the concerns of the Reformation in such a way that their accuracy and effectiveness may prove to be legitimate and welcome also for the Catholic Church. One is all the more obliged to expose oneself to the brilliant critique Kueng directs at Kaesemann, and through him at a considerable portion of Protestant exegesis. This critique touches upon every search for a canon in the canon. According to Kueng, what was thought of as a standard of interpretation becomes for Kaesemann the material principle of selection. The latter's proving of the spirits in the New Testament signifies that he does not want to hear the Gospel from those "spirits declared to be evil." To Kueng it is entirely questionable "that he [Kaesemann] himself can know where things do not concern themselves with the Gospel." Exegesis alone, says Kueng, cannot offer a sufficient basis for the total undertaking. The real supportive foundation here is "some final option" which can no longer be made rationally comprehensible. Two previously quoted sentences bear repeating: "Is not this a position in which one can hardly cite reasons that could prevent someone else from hitting upon a *different* option, and on the basis of another ... pre-understanding exegetically discovering another middle and another Gospel?" [111] "The bold program of finding a 'canon in the canon' demands nothing else than this: to be more Biblical than the Bible, more New Testamently than the New Testament, more evangelical than the Gospel, and even more Pauline than Paul. Radical earnestness is the intention, radical dissolution is the result ... the true Paul is the entire Paul, and the true New Testament is the entire New Testament." Thus the bold program leads to "subjective arbitrariness." [112]

In the light of this annihilating critique one is moved to ask: What does Kueng say about the contradictions which historical-critical exegesis detects in the New Testament? One will seek in vain for a new helpful direction. As critical as Kueng is in making judgments about the canon in the canon, just so uncritically, on the other hand, he admits to the correctness of historical-critical exegesis. The New Testament according to Kueng is really a *complexio oppositorum.* [113] But that will do no harm because the Roman Catholic Church understands how "to embrace these opposites in a good sense." At this juncture, where to a certain extent ecclesiology rescues soteriology together with Christology, [114] Biblical and Reformation theology will have to divorce itself from him.

4. Appendix: The Church Historians

In conclusion and to round things off, we will take a glance at the church historians. In a certain sense they are more neutral observers and advisers insofar as the length of the historical tradition lifts them out of a too-contemporary involvement. The essay by *K. Aland* unfortunately is too historically-phenomenologically styled. He underlines the indubitable fact that every denomination, in keeping with its self-understanding, develops a real working canon for itself. This canon goes "right through the middle of the formal canon, yes, right through the middle of individual [books of] Scripture." He considers it possible that all churches arrive at a common canon that works for them. The assumption for this is the "discussion of the proper principles for the selection out of the formal canon and the interpretation of the canon that has thus come into being, with the aim of arriving at a common, factual canon." [115] Since we here again are face to face with the conviction and the theme of the well-known "canon in the canon," we will not pursue the subject further.

Hans von Campenhausen, in contrast to his Muenster colleague, rejects acceptance of a specific theological formula (such as, for example, "what teaches Christ") or a basic thought (as, for example, the proclamation of justification) as a canon in the canon. Decisive also for him is the experience which the "Christians of the primitive church and of all times" have had with the New Testament. There is here, he states, a spiritual unity with which one certainly must constantly engage himself. Christians have again and again found the "one meaning" in the New Testament. [116]

One can see that also the advice of the church historians is tied to their systematic position. They, too, cannot escape the tension between the differing poles: spiritual experience of the congregation on the one hand, and modern critical exegesis on the other—between the real canon created out of many factors at work in spiritual life and the methodologically absolute and exclusive "canon in the canon."

5. Summary

In the essays of Kaesemann's collection we have seen a representative cross section of contemporary German exegesis and systematics which has acquainted us with the authoritative exponents of the historical-critical method. Other authors, to be sure, may still change its style but not its basic precepts. The results may now be summarized.

1. The exegetes can no longer conceive of the New Testament as a unit, but merely as a collection of various testimonies which are contradictory and have varying degrees of validity.

2. For them it is an established fact that the formal canon cannot be equated with the Word of God. To the present day Semler's distinction between Scripture and Word of God has indisputable significance. This thesis and the claim that there are contradictions in the New Testament complement and support each other.

3. In view of the described situation, exegetes and systematicians have been searching for more than 200 years for the canon in the canon, i. e., for the binding Word of divine authority. This two-century undertaking has failed, since no one is in the position of convincingly and meaningfully defining a canon in the canon.

4. Since each theologian conceives of the canon in the canon differently, and since this is done on the basis of an assumption no longer questioned (i. e., by free choice), uncontrolled subjectivity has the last word concerning what should have divine authority.

5. To the degree that systematicians reject a canon in the canon in order to maintain freedom for the Scriptures, they must search for the unity of Scripture outside of Scripture, because none of them can surmount the historical-critical method with its contradictory results. As for Roman Catholics, they take refuge in the official teaching office of the church, which makes the

decisions concerning Scripture; on the Protestant side, appeal is made to the spiritual experience of the congregation, which produces a unity in contrast to Scripture research and thereby in practice comes to stand above Scripture.

Thus the use of the higher-critical method has put us into a monstrous hole. The downfall here described proved to be inescapable. What the real Word of God is became more and more nebulous.

It must be clear to every intelligent person that one cannot go on this way. For it is impossible that human subjectivity will come to agreement as to what has divine authority and where God is speaking. Through the use of the higher-critical method we have been far removed from the directive of Jesus: "Search the Scriptures, for in them ye think ye have eternal life; and they are they which testify of Me" (John 5:39) and far removed from the apostles, the true church fathers, and Luther. For all of them "It is written" was the clinching argument.

The subtle net woven by the higher-critical method resulted in a new Babylonian captivity of the church. It became more and more isolated from the living stream of Bible proclamation, and therefore more and more uncertain and blind both as to its own course and also in relation to its influence toward the outside. On the other hand, on the part of those who were working historically-critically, i. e., the theological scholars, there occurred not only a dissociation from the Bible—which at the same time implied recourse to other thoughts—but also a dissociation from congregations, which before and after considered the Scriptures as a unity and fashioned their lives accordingly.

One point deserves to be especially emphasized. The representatives of the higher-critical method have given sharp opposition to the orthodox thoughts concerning the *perspicuitas* (clarity) and *sufficientia* (sufficiency) of the Scriptures.[117] They have obscured the clarity by their "proof" of contradictions in the Bible, and they have clung to and deepened the obscurity by means of their fruitless search for a canon in the canon. They have undermined the sufficiency of the Scriptures by claiming that the historical-critical work was necessary in order to comprehend the Scriptures. To the degree that their views asserted themselves, a division set in between Scripture and congregation. However, the matter has not ended with Scripture. Since through Scripture we meet God and learn to know Him, therefore by invalidating the clarity and sufficiency of Scripture, they have also destroyed the certainty of faith. If it is uncertain *where* the living God is speaking, then I no longer know *who* is speaking. With that, confidence has become impossible, and one can understand the ignorance of those who came to Jesus with the question, "What must I do to inherit eternal life?"

It would be a big mistake to blame this development of things on the incompetence of the *methodizers*. Rather, it is the fault of the *method* they have selected. The above exposition showed that the method had to fail because it was not suited to the subject. We can now accept as a proved fact that Scripture itself does not offer a canon in the canon, but that the latter is exacted forcibly and against its will. What kind of a horrible providence would it be for God to let us search for a binding canon so long and so despairingly with only the result of increasing uncertainty! The constant witness of Scripture confirms that certainty is the goal of God's love and the content of the prayer: "Order my steps in Thy Word, and let not any iniquity have dominion over me," [118] while uncertainty originates out of opposition to God. If there should really be a canon in the canon, then not only would Scripture have to be divorced from the Word of God, but also Christ from the Scriptures, the Holy Ghost from the Scriptures, and the one Christ of Scripture from the other Christ of Scripture. The light of a new docetism [119] would then fall on the event of the Incarnation and on certain parts of Scripture. The canon in the canon would move into dangerous proximity to being a mere idea; the contingency of history would, to say the least, be attacked. For the impartial hearer of the Word, those would obviously be nonsensical results.

After the higher-critical method, for all practical purposes, has arrived at the end of a blind alley, we are faced with the responsiblity of finding a different method of Biblical inquiry and scholarly study—one better suited to its subject. The insight that 200 years of custom and theological education have pointed us in another direction, and that for this reason the prospects are poor, should not keep us from finding a better method. Neither should the fact that criticizing what is at hand is easier than making a positive recommendation for a new beginning.

III.

THE NECESSITY OF A HISTORICAL-BIBLICAL METHOD

1. A Dogmatic "Prejudice"?

a) How It Differs from the General Historical Method: No Compelling Principle of Analogy

After the empirical end of the higher-critical method, we are faced with an immense task. This task is to develop an exegetical method which is in accord with revelation in the form of the Holy Scriptures. This includes surmounting the philosophically based cleavage between Scripture and the Word of God introduced by Semler and his colleagues. This implies nothing less than vanquishing English deism, French skepticism, and the German Enlightenment in the domain of theology.

Decisive for the outcome will be the point where we begin. If the beginning is made at the wrong place, the best intentions are doomed to failure.

Also the critics of the hitherto prevailing method are agreed that any new method to be employed must have a historical basis.[120] A historical method? Yes! A critical method? "No!" or "Caution!" is the watchword. But can we here be concerned simply with "the historical method"?

Secular historiography may, in fact, have certain proved methodological principles of long standing.[121] However, its subject matter is what took place among people, was observed by human eyes, and was produced by human thoughts. Perhaps the individual historian is really a Christian and even sees development of a divine plan in his area of scholarship. Or perhaps he has some other religious conviction and sees it verified in what his studies reveal. It would, of course, be most absurd to try to isolate the individual researcher from his religious—or pseudoreligious—

convictions. However, whether in the former or the latter case, his questioning will always be different from that of the interpreter of Scripture. That is, the historian inquires about the activity or condition of people, i. e., his concern is anthropological. The Biblical scholar, however, inquires about the activity of God and the story of His relationship with man, i. e., his concern is theological.

This simple observation has a far-reaching implication. While the secular historiographer must apply the basic principle that all events possess an equivalent (analogy) which makes classification with comparable events possible, the Biblical scholar *dare* not persist in using this principle of analogy in all cases. For it is just what happens *only once*—the thing that cannot be analogized—that we may anticipate as the living God's way of acting. Were one to maintain that God always and exclusively comes to the fore concealed in human activity that the world can decipher, then this claim would set limitations to the divinity of God. Therefore, what regular historiography demands is expressly forbidden by the scholarly responsibility of theological study. Suspending the compelling principle of analogy, accordingly, represents a basic difference between general historiographic methodology and theological methodology.[122]

Now it is in the execution of what has been said, in line with previous experience, that we look for or claim a specific activity of God in specific circumstances of our history. For this reason, with a certain amount of justification, the "historicity of revelation" is again and again made valid, although it would be an unforgivable error again to misunderstand this expression in the sense of general history. Nevertheless, it is clear that what was said above as generally pertaining to God's activity must also be valid as it pertains to historical events in which, we presume, such activity of God finds expression. But it is especially valid when concrete material is at hand which claims to be divinely revealed, that is, in the Holy Scriptures. The different questioning by the regular historian and by the theologian (of course, also by the historical theologian) implies different attitudes toward the material. To this extent the Bible is a book *sui generis* (peculiar to itself), even from the theological-methodological starting point. A Cannae and a Caudine subjugation[123] of theology has been the result wherever, in applying the historical-critical method, this basic principle has been allowed to be weakened and made unworkable.

An example may be briefly cited. When the regular historiographer uses the Bible in his inquiry, he will do this according to his normal working methods, i. e., he will treat the Bible like any other document—and he will likely gain something from it. His results, however, will have a character that is purely historical, not theological. In the exercise of his assumed right he will occasionally state his doubts; for example, regarding the incarnation of Jesus he may point out that something like this is a sheer impossibility. He would, however, exceed his methodological right if he were to maintain outright that the Incarnation did not take place or that it did not happen in the way it was recorded. In the event—which he need not even consider— that the Bible really is the written deposit of what is divinely revealed and authorized, he could say nothing about God and would probably have falsely evaluated a good part of the Biblical content. The theologian is different. He must methodologically begin with the assumption that a given event here is possible, and therefore he must ensure an openness to the methodological principle which will not hastily and insolently curtail divine revelation at any place. It is just this which requires a "wide-angle" methodological attitude which must not prematurely exclude certain possibilities. That this has happened is reason enough to rebuke the historical-critical method.[124] Therefore the historical-critical method is to be replaced by a historical-Biblical one.[125]

b) The Sovereignty of God

Thus far we have proceeded from the methodological principle that in the investigation of Scripture enforced analogy has to be abandoned and that the method must be adapted so as everywhere to permit the possibility of divine revelation. A second consideration is now added to the above. If one is to treat the concept of the sovereignty of God seriously, then it would have to be a trait of this sovereignty to reveal itself whenever and wherever He should wish to do so. As is well known, such a formulation did enter the confessional documents of the Reformation.[126] As a result of this, we should recognize that it is not our findings that determine what has divine authority, nor does the concession of possibilities suffice to establish a pertinent theology. Rather, one must be alert as to where divine revelation desires to make itself heard. The next step would be to enter this area obediently, and from there to let a venturesome faith continue its search along those paths to which revelation directs us.

As can be seen, with our first considerations as to methodology we are already in the middle of theological action. Thus it was a big mistake that the higher-critical method for a long time claimed that it could and should approach the texts "objectively" and in an "unprejudiced" way. The statement that one must inquire into a theological subject with methods independent of theology, i. e., with "atheological" methods, is a contradiction in itself and just the opposite of what is needed. Rather, it is of concern that theology again reflect thoroughly and responsibly upon the systematic assumptions of exegesis, that it resolutely concentrate on its own methodology and clarify it as much as possible. For the statement, "I am not ashamed of the Gospel" (Rom. 1:16) is valid also with regard to methodology. It would indeed be strange if scholarly inquiry in rendering account of subjects related to divine revelation should be subject to the same rules of method that apply to those subjects which have to do with nature or human history.[127]

Let us return to the subject of the sovereignty of God, which of and by itself determines where, when, and how He wishes to reveal Himself. One should not let oneself be frightened here by recalling the late nominalism of William of Ockham or of Gabriel Biel (which, by the way, also extended its roots to Luther).[128] Admittedly, nominalism did teach free choice in God's activity in a one-sided and exaggerated way. However, its idea concerning the freedom of God which is restricted only by itself remains valuable and correct just here where we are concerned with Him who reveals Himself freely.

Theology has to feel its way and in completely surrendered obedience occupy the ground that divine revelation designates to it. This means the methodological obligation of accepting revelation. Every critical attempt at establishing something in advance is here out of place. Methodologically speaking, it would mean that man in this encounter possesses a right of control, a right of intellectual reservation, and even the right to shape the encounter with God on the same level, so to speak, as an exchange partner. Obviously, this would be something impossible, because again it would be an attempt to limit the divinity of God in advance.

As for method, we are here moving correctly if we cling to the word of Jesus: "If any man will do His will [i. e., the will of Him who has sent Him, namely God], he shall know of the doctrine, whether it be of God or whether I speak of Myself" (John 7:17). By the way, this is the only methodological principle Jesus offered for the sure gaining of understanding in the area of revelation. In an irreversible way it deduces understanding from obedience, confirms the above-mentioned idea that revelation and obedience, not revelation and critique, are corresponding terms, and proclaims the failure of every attempt to acquire an orderly grasp of revelation with the yardstick of analogy or any other attempted standard. Thus it has been stated correctly: *credo, ut intellegam* (I believe in order to understand), not *credo, quia intellego* (I believe because I understand). Therefore it must be clear to us that right doctrine presumes right living, also on the part of the individual theologian. Without being born again, we remain as ignorant as Nicodemus.[129]

We pursue the subject of the sovereignty of God a little further. To begin with, it is simple to establish that Holy Scripture clearly articulates this subject.[130] On the other hand, however, value is placed on the Incarnation (God's Son becoming flesh), and this is interpreted as though God has therewith disposed of all sovereignty in such a way that He is now entirely human, i. e., that He may be perceived critically. As a further conclusion it is claimed that a *sacrificium intellectus,* a sacrifice of critically evaluating human reason, is opposed to God. However, it is basically not a matter of the *sacrificium intellectus* but of the *sacrificium superbiae,* the sacrifice of pride. Only the Revelator can declare authoritatively how the Incarnation is here to be understood. Otherwise our human pride would again have taken the helm through some theological stroke of fortune. The result would be, in the first place, the justification of our human reason through the Incarnation alone and not through the cross, and thereafter there would be a loss of certainty. No honest theologian can want that.[131] The word of Jesus, "If the Son, therefore, shall make you free, ye shall be free indeed" (John 8:36) makes it very clear that He remains the Son and is Himself free. The repeated assurance, "Thy faith hath made thee whole," as in the story of the Samaritan leper (Luke 17:19), is intended to invest faith with legitimacy and power, thus to ensure certainty. On the basis of the Biblical evidence, the goal of the Incarnation is certainty, not confusion. Our method must not run counter to this objective.

A further step resulting from the idea of the sovereignty of God is the recognition of the statement that the only binding and underived interpretation of revelation is revelation itself. That is to say, in the words of the fathers of the Reformation: Scripture interprets itself—*Scriptura sui ipsius interpres.* Therefore also their cry: *ad fontem*—back to the source! The self-interpretation of Scripture is most profoundly connected with its goal of producing certainty.

In a unique way this was formulated by Luther, whom we quote here at some length: "Who is the judge by whom a question is decided when the statements of the fathers conflict? For here one must reach a conclusion in accordance with the judgment of Scripture, and this cannot be done if we do not give first place to Scripture in everything attributed to the fathers, so that it [Scripture] itself, through itself, is the most certain, the most easily accessible, the most easily understood—it, which interprets itself, which verifies, judges, and illuminates all statements of all." And a little later Luther adds: "I desire that Scripture alone should be queen."[132]

What are the consequences of this method? To begin with, it is suggested that from the oneness of the Revelator one may conclude that there is unity in revelations. It must be permissible to take a reference from one part of Scripture and compare it with another. To be sure, clinging to God's sovereignty does not offhand prevent anyone from assuming that in the course of various revelations also contradiction has a place. However, in view of the aim to attain obedience and certainty through revelation, one will have to adjust the *method* toward first of all seeking agreement and unity in what has been revealed, and at the same time to take up the indications in the latter. Whenever revelation itself does not note any recognizable differences, one is obliged, methodologically speaking, to follow its lead.

From the constant criticism of the "concordance method" we must proceed methodologically to a well-grounded suspicion over against the "dissonance method," i. e., the intention to stress contradictions and disagreements. The method of thinking in theological "blocks," for example, proves itself to be on the wrong methodological road. However, we must pay very close attention to the direction and manner of development which revelation itself takes or aspires to. Accordingly, we must not without further ado reclaim for the New Covenant that which was said in the Old Covenant. Finally there emerges for the individual interpreter the demand to base all his explanations on Scripture itself and to permit himself to be permeated more and more by the Spirit of Scripture.[133]

Attention must still be directed to a consequence which, however, should not become an independent foundation of the method. A certain subjectivity necessarily attaches to every theology. "For we know in part, and we prophesy in part. . . . Now I know in part" (1 Cor. 13:9, 12). In the present earthly situation no theologian will be able to maintain that he can see everything, and that he can see it all correctly. Just therefore a thorough theory of method will be intent, on the one hand, to maintain and sharpen the consciousness of subjective limitation and, on the other hand, gratefully to make use of every counterbalance to this. There is no more dependable control than the Scriptures. From this point of view one will again have to cultivate a healthy suspicion about every fragmentation of Scripture, which in turn would serve as the entering wedge for high-handed subjectivity. Because theology is necessarily subjective, one may not therefore frivolously give up the most powerful organ of control— Scripture—to subjectivity.

c) The Role of the Congregation's Spiritual Experience

We have not as yet touched upon a third train of thought, which complements the two previous ideas concerning freedom from the principle of analogy and concerning the sovereignty of God. It concerns a fact which a contemporary theory of method must not overlook, namely, the often-mentioned spiritual experience of the congregation of Jesus.[134]

It is freely admitted that we consider this range of ideas less forceful than the two previous arguments. There is much that deters us from placing too much weight on this principle. There is the reminder of the "experience" of the sects and false teachers who found support in it. There were many "experiences" in the pre-Reformation church with its saints, and these have reached down to the present time. There are emotional "experiences" in the extreme Pentecostal groups. There is the often misunderstood "Biblical Christ" of Kaehler [19th-century theological professor at Bonn and Halle], or the "Christ no more according to the flesh" of Bultmann, whereby they evaded the question of historical truth.[135] Finally, recall the prophesied apostasy of the church to the amazing Antichrist in the Revelation of St. John (chs. 17 and 18).

We cannot, therefore, follow the precedent of those systematicians who turned precisely to spiritual experience to stem the tide of historical-critical exegesis. Nevertheless, we had occasion to be astonished at the wide front in which they, in spite of their sympathy for the higher-critical method, attested to the correctness of that experience. Nor will one be able to refute the verdict of church historians that the believing and obedient congregation has always experienced all of Scripture as a unity. Today this could possibly be substantiated by the history of the groups that make up the Evangelical Alliance.

The value of such experience lies first of all in this, that the methodological assumptions of freedom from analogy and of the sovereignty of God have, to a degree, been given a "place in life" and are not presented simply as ideas. They are, rather, a reflection of what the congregation experiences as it carries out its revealed mission. However, that is not all. In particular, there is here a reinforcement of the conviction concerning the unity of Scripture, which we have above carefully been able to deduce from the idea of sovereignty. In the third place, we should be open to the consideration that such experience is not only the somewhat mechanical consequence of using the Scriptures but is effected by the Spirit of revelation. Thus we have already arrived at the inner witness of the Holy Spirit *(testimonium internum Spiritus Sancti),* which indeed testifies to the revelatory nature of Scripture, its unity, and its lively action, in keeping with the understanding of the congregation.[136]

To rule out any misunderstanding, let it be clearly stated that in no wise is there any intention to play down the importance of the witness of the Holy Spirit. At all events, our first concern is to lead people to listen to the Word of God, letting faith and the seal of the Holy Spirit follow in normal order (Rom. 10:14-17). Further, since there is all about us today a new intoxicating fanaticism *(Schwaermerei)* which knows no boundaries,[137] we should be extremely careful about everything that is subjective and difficult to think through responsibly.[138] "If there be any virtue . . . think on these things" (Phil. 4:8).

d) Summary

We summarize: In view of the demand for a historical method of Scripture interpretation, our preliminary considerations revealed that for God's revelation we cannot just apply "the" historical method generally used in historiography. Rather, if one wants to allow even for the possibility of divine revelation, one must decide at the start to put aside the principle of analogy, which permits no exceptions, and obediently give way to the sovereignty of God. The "spiritual experience of the congregation" is for the researcher somewhat of a road sign for the correctness of this procedure.

Since the preliminary decisions, which we have previously mentioned and which are unavoidable, already have dogmatic character, Scriptural interpretation is impossible without dogmatic prejudice in this sense. Rather, we must become conscious of the fact that the methodology to be followed has from the very beginning extreme theological significance and accordingly must be constructed with theological awareness. Such a course does not result from a thirst for power or from the eccentricity of the theologians, but it is demanded by the subject itself, revelation. Included in the requirements is an obedient life-style on the part of the scholar. In consideration of the particularity of the subject and in contrast to the general historical method, we are calling the procedure here proposed the *historical-Biblical method.*[139]

2. The Problem of Scriptural Authority

a) Scripture and Revelation

The problem of Scriptural authority is the first case that can be more exactly defined in which the above-mentioned "dogmatic prejudice" is prominent and must prove its effectiveness. Many a person may, perhaps, have expected the authority of Scripture to be discussed *prior to* the ideas explained above, and indeed, it would have been methodologically possible to present a positive statement on revelation in that manner. However, such a quick approach to Scripture seemed a little hurried to us, namely on the basis of the fact the Scripture sometimes represents a later stage in the process of revelation. For example, the Gospels follow upon the preaching of Jesus. Thus ultimately the Scriptures stand between the first stage of revelation—for the most part, God's speaking—and the later handing down of what has been revealed. On the basis of the "wide-angle" stance of methodology, previously established, it is accordingly appropriate to focus on the Scriptures as a particular procedure in the process of revelation *after* the general presuppositions of method have been set forth.

In this we find ourselves in agreement with the fathers. The classic position for this has been formulated by Hollaz, who stated in his *Examen:* [140] "Christian theology is based on the most certain principle of knowledge, namely on divine revelation—in fact, according to the present situation of the church, it is based on the divine revelation transmitted to us as contained in the writings of the prophets and apostles. For this reason the *absolute* first, all-inclusive principle of theology is: What God has revealed, that is infallibly true. The *relative,* and for the present day first, principle of theology is: What the Holy Scriptures teach, that is infallibly certain." [141]

Now we must immediately face the frequently voiced objection [142] which is based on the difference that often exists between the first oral stage of revelation and the second stage, the establishment of the written text; or in terms of Hollaz' concepts, the difference between the absolute first principle and the relative first principle. This difference is evaluated in various ways. It is said, for example, that the many words in the Scriptures are all intended to lead to the One Final Word (Karl Barth) [143] and that therefore the many individual words are in themselves not of such great concern. Or it is said that the words of Scripture are not only conditioned in their relation to a Final Word, but that they are not even germane to the subject they treat. The latter interpretation is represented, for example, by R. Bultmann in a very pointed way: "It is not only a matter of the relativity of the word, but it also concerns the fact that no man—not even St. Paul—discourses always and only on the subject at hand. In him also other spirits than the *pneuma Christou* find expression." [144]

Therewith the problem of the "canon in the canon" appears again, which we have examined and rejected in the previous chapter. Here we therefore want to discuss only the effects of those viewpoints as they pertain to the authority of Scripture. It is recognized that when Scripture, in regard to revelation, is viewed *only* as witness to revelation, its authority becomes deficient. In the search for the true, binding revelation, Scripture appears only as a means of access, as a step which basically can be surmounted. In the unfolding of the canon problem we again meet the viewpoint which has already placed itself *above* Scripture, and that with logical consistency. Therefore we may not treat the difference between Scripture and God's first oral revelation in this manner.

But what now? First, it must be noted that often the first stage of revelation is already the written form. This is true, for example, for the entire epistolary literature of the New Testament, and also for the Revelation of John and the Acts of the Apostles; the same is true in the Old Testament for the *Ketubim* (Job, Psalms, Proverbs, Ecclesiastes, and Song of Solomon), for the Book of the Covenant (Ex. 24:7), and parts of the Prophets (Jer. 36; Is. 8:16). If one were to be really serious in making a qualitative distinction between Scripture as witness of revelation and revelation itself, then one would again have to divide Scriptural content into two parts. Second, in making this distinction one runs into difficulties with the Biblical and traditional interpretation of the inspiration of Scripture. On a purely logical basis it is not justified—in the event that the Scriptures really are inspired by the Holy Spirit—again to downgrade their authority by accepting them *merely* as a witness. In the third place, we must note that the Scriptures—also in those instances where a recognizably later stage is presented in the record, as for example the gospels in relation to the preaching of

Jesus—are the only means whereby what has been revealed was established and handed down. But in the fourth place—and here we run into the most decisive point in methodology—the above-sketched attempt at a qualitative downgrading of Scripture comes into conflict with Scripture itself.

b) What the Scriptures Say About Themselves

If we want to remain faithful to the principles of methodology suggested above, then it follows, especially in keeping with the concept of the sovereignty of God, that only Scripture itself can say in a binding way what authority it claims and has. For reasons that have been explained we had determined upon a "wide-angle" methodology, upon an "as if"[145] theology, which alone is appropriate to revelation because thereby revelation retains its freedom. Since the Bible is the earliest, most universal, and most basic document which shapes for us as Christians an attainable revelation, we must proceed from what has here been said.

How does Jesus, the Son of God and "the Truth" (John 14:6; 5:19 ff.; 20:31), view the Scriptures? How do the apostles, who speak therein, view the Bible? Like most Jewish teachers, Jesus based His statements on the Old Testament Scriptures.[146] Practically and theoretically, He attached even greater value to the Scriptures and took them more seriously than did these teachers. This may be seen in His sharpening of the Torah in the Sermon on the Mount, in the restoration of the Torah over against the "tradition of the elders" (Matt. 15:1 ff.), and also in His clarification in Matt. 5:17-18: "Think not that I am come to destroy the Law or the Prophets; I am not come to destroy, but to fulfill. For verily I say unto you, till heaven and earth pass, one jot or one tittle shall in no wise pass from the Law, till all be fulfilled." Even when in the opinion of His opponents He broke the Sabbath, He appealed to the authority of the Scriptures (Matt. 12:3 ff.; Mark 3:1 ff.). In any controversy Jesus made the decision on the basis of Scriptural quotations.[147]

These are all well-known facts. In connection with our subject, however, three further observations become important. The first of these shows a surprising measure of reliance on the exact wording of the Torah, as well as the *Ketubim*.[148] Two examples of this may be cited from His controversies. In the discussion with the

Sadducees, Jesus proves that the resurrection conforms to Scripture and therefore is a reality. His proof is taken from God's self-disclosure in Ex. 3:6: "I am the God of . . . Abraham, the God of Isaac, and the God of Jacob." He concludes from these words that God, as God of the living, causes the respective individuals to experience a resurrection. Again, in discussion with the Pharisees, Jesus proves the divine Sonship of the Messiah from the words of David in Ps. 110:1: "The Lord said unto my Lord, sit Thou at My right hand. . . ."

This very passage leads to the second observation. It reveals that Jesus not only trusts the psalms literally, accepting also the indicated authorship, but also views them as prophetic-Messianic declarations, similar to the way this was done at Qumran.[149] So the historical-critical designation of the psalms as the "prayerbook" of Israel was not His view.

The third observation is that Jesus' literal understanding of a Scripture passage also offered opportunity for Him to tie in a prophetic-parabolic or even a spiritual-allegorical interpretation. This may be seen, for example, in His judgment of the nowadays highly controversial Book of Jonah. Jesus here not only accepts as a self-evident fact Jonah's stay in the belly of the great fish, but He also prophetically sees in the fate of the prophet His own anticipated parallel experience.[150]

The sermons of Peter[151] as well as the letters of Paul[152] make it clear that the apostles shared Jesus' interpretation of Scripture—as is obviously expected of His disciples. Beyond that, the New Testament bears witness to two developments which in our context are of utmost interest. In the first place—and this was probably addressed to the Gentile Christian area, where the validity of Scripture was subject to attacks from completely different currents in intellectual history—it is emphasized that *all Scripture* is the activity and result of the Holy Ghost (the so-called *theopneustia),* that is, the authors produced nothing merely human, but "borne by the Holy Ghost" spoke with God as the Source.[153] In the second place, the New Testament authors constantly assure us that they themselves are now writing reliably and as persons filled with the Holy Ghost. Paul as well as Peter and John use this approach.[154] The Book of Revelation underscores this solemnly, applying it to every word.[155] The affirmation in the introduction of Luke [156] is even surpassed by the silent yet significant manner in which Matthew and John, by means of Old Testament captions or initial statements, give their gospels the authority of the old Holy Scriptures.[157] In the case of St. Mark we must assume the same thing.[158]

Let us take special note of a passage which is particularly enlightening. It concerns 2 Peter 3:15 f., in which Peter supports his admonition with the letters of Paul. While admitting that they are difficult to understand, Peter gives them the same status as "the other Scriptures," i.e., the Old Testament. Peter notes that God [159] had given Paul this wisdom. It cannot be expressed more clearly that the New Testament apostolate and the New Testament prophetic office possess the same authority as their predecessors in the Old Testament. Since God's concluding and final word was spoken "by His Son," surpassing prophets and angels (Heb. 1:1 ff.), the primary stress has even been shifted to the New Testament.[160]

In view of all this, the following conclusions must be reached with regard to the authority of Scripture: Our starting point was the methodological insight that, at least initially, we must let revelation determine its own limits. Consequently revelation defines itself. For Christians the first point of contact is Holy Scripture. We have seen that Scripture considers itself as revelation: All Scripture is declared to be the work of the holy Revelator, the Spirit of God. Thereafter we may consider Scripture in a limiting way as *one* stage in the process of revelation—to the degree that, as in the Gospels, the Scriptural report follows upon a revelatory occurrence. Yet it is nothing other and no less than *revelation.* An unduly inquisitive knowledge of the original revelation in opposition to a witness thereto which for us is understandably sketchy is just as inadmissible as a correction of the *Deus revelatus* (revealed God) by means of a conjectured *Deus absconditus* (concealed God). The implication of this methodological insight for the study of exegesis is obvious. Ever since the Enlightenment the statement that Scripture *contains* divine revelation has prevailed and has become a leading dogma. But we have to rule it out. The true statement reads: "Scripture *is* revelation."[161]

c) The Inspiration of the Scriptures

Almost unawares we have herewith been led into the realm of the revered doctrine of inspiration, which is again a burning issue. If the authority of Scripture is at the base of the knotty problem of the methodological strife in theology, then the questions and decisions pretaining to the authority of Scripture are all tied to the doctrine of inspiration. With the term "the doctrine of inspiration" we designate the formulated teaching that Scripture is the result of the activity of the Holy Spirit ("inspired"). While the fact is established by Scripture beyond any doubt (see above), the doctrine, i. e., the closer delineation, is a theological responsibility which must be established *prior to* the exegesis or interpretation of Scripture; that is to say, it is really in the area of theological methodology. For it is obvious that exegetical conclusions will vary greatly, depending on whether the exegete assumes a comprehensive doctrine of inspiration, a partial one, or no inspiration at all. On a subject as sensitive as this, one should, as a start, read the church fathers, who after all also have a relationship to the spiritual experience of the congregation of Jesus.

Even before the Reformers it was common conviction and established doctrine that the Holy Scriptures as a whole represent an authority that is not open to criticism.[162] Augustine, for example, viewed Scripture as originating by dictation from the Holy Spirit. Those who struggled against the papal curia and the power of the representatives of canonical law again fell back more strongly to the Scriptures as the governing norm. One must, however, be careful in assuming a *sola Scriptura* (Scripture alone) principle in the late Middle Ages on the part of the nominalist teachers of Luther.[163] Gabriel Biel, for example, still recognized extra-Biblical church tradition as a second authority, and stated: "There are many other things which by all means must be believed and done, but about which the Bible says nothing." [164]

A fundamental change came to predominate with Luther in the course of his studies. The *sola Scriptura* precept became his banner and his arsenal in the struggle with the papal church. Now all tradition of the church which could not be substantiated by the Bible was excluded or minimized. And beyond all doubt, Luther considered the *entire* Bible to be inspired. In this connection it is doubtful, methodologically speaking, that one should here give consideration to Luther's critical remarks concerning the books of James, Jude, Hebrews, and Revelation, because these comments touch upon a completely different subject, namely, whether these writings even belong to the canon. However, all books that do belong to the canon have authority and are accepted as being inspired.

What this signified for Luther is evident with exemplary clarity from his themes for debate under the title *De fide* (concerning faith) of 1535. No. 59 states: "For we are not all apostles, who by the certain decree of God have been sent to us as infallible teachers." No. 60 reads: "Therefore not they, but we, who are without such a decree, may err and fall in faith."[165] According to this, the apostles in their statements in Scripture are infallible because God has sent them to us as teachers. Inspiration here aims at the infallibility and the certainty of the faith which depends on this Word. Inspiration lifts Scripture above all human utterances as well as above all access by human criticism and, notwithstanding the fact that it was written by men, gives it the attributes and the preeminence of divine discourse. "When God speaks through man, that is a far different thing than man himself speaking."[166] From this Luther concludes: "So nothing but the divine words should be the first principles of Christians, but the words of all men are conclusions which are derived therefrom and must be led back to them and verified by them."[167] From here we arrive in a straight line at the convictions and formulations of late orthodoxy[168] after Luther, where we read in the *Examen* of Hollaz or the *Epitome* of Calixt: "Whatever Holy Scripture teaches is unfailingly true," supplemented and supported by the thesis: "In the most exact sense of the concept the Holy Scriptures are the Word of God."[169]

Thus both in the pre-Reformation church and in the church of the Reformation, as well as in the Roman Catholic Church until the Enlightenment, we consistently find the interpretation that Holy Scripture in totality, i. e., in its handed-down canonical form, is inspired. Insofar as one views Scripture as the Word of God, that is, His revelation, this is so to speak self-evident.

Now, however, new questions arise. In the first place: What are the facts about the gathering together of the canon, since there is in the canon no direct statement concerning its scope? In the second place: What are the facts about the relationship between "man's word" and "God's Word" in Scripture? In the third place: How is the problem of "contradictions" or "scientific errors" in Scripture to be explained? In the fourth place: To what degree, then, is inspiration valid in the individual case?

d) The Scope of the Canon

The coming into being and growth of the canon was, as is well known, a painful and difficult struggle in the church, especially with Jewish elements, over a period of several centuries. It is generally held that it was not concluded until A.D. 367, when Athanasius published his Easter letter. When we speak of "growth," that could readily be misunderstood. For, to be more exact, it was not so much a process of growth, but rather a process of elimination. The number of writings considered for canonicity became smaller and smaller. Out of the abundance of earliest Christian literature not only the apocalyptic books, which people enjoyed reading, such as Enoch, the Ascension of Moses, the Martyrdom of Isaiah, and others,[170] but also writings of highest apostolic claim, such as the Kerygma of Peter, the Gospel of Thomas, the false Acts of the Apostles, or the Didache, were all pushed aside as being of secondary quality. The same fate befell the Letter to Laodicea[171] and other letters attributed to St. Paul, as well as literature of students of the apostles as early as the first-century First Letter of Bishop Clement of Rome, still highly esteemed today. Even critical scholars credit the church with using a most rigid standard, in line with the circumstances of that day, in making its selection. Even many a genuine statement of Jesus might possibly have been eliminated in the process.[172]

These well-known facts force us to conclude that the canonical selection was limited to the earliest and most dependable manuscripts. A distinctive peculiarity of the procedure is that it was not prophetically commanded by a specific statement at a specific time. The standard of selection was, rather, the widest approval in all congregations, and then only after thorough explanation and repeated discussion of many manuscripts over a period of years, even centuries. Further, it cannot be denied that the spiritual experience of the congregation in all succeeding ages became possible with and by means of this canon.

But even though we were to make the most beautiful and eloquent statements about the early church's selection, we would still have said nothing about God's authority in determining the canon. Besides, we wanted to remain cautious as soon as spiritual experience begins to assert itself as a principle of cognition with regard to revelation. When it comes to method, we must proceed more flawlessly and be sure of our ground, that is to say, also now we must gain the approach and the direction of our cognition out of revelation itself. Thereby we can indeed designate an "inner boundary" for establishing a canon, namely, in the sense that all the writings now in the canon—we are disregarding the apocryphal books for the moment [173]—either themselves claim to be revelation or are given this standing through the testimony of other writings in the canon. That is, if we proceed from the concept of revelation in the form of Scripture, we may assume that there is no Scripture *in* the canon which is *without* canonical quality.

This, however, still does not clarify the "outer boundary," that is, the question as to whether all canonically necessary writings have really attained canonical standing. Here we must rely on an indirect conclusion. In the event that a canonically *necessary* writing is missing, then God would have led the church right up to the present day into at least an incomplete and dangerous path, perhaps even into a wrong path. Only if the missing writing were to be discovered would we then be justified in speaking about a saving revelation. Accordingly, it is most unlikely that such a writing is missing; as to methodology, the subject should be set aside.

Exactly at this point we must methodologically refer to the orthodox teaching about the *sufficientia* (sufficiency) of Scripture. Without the sufficiency of Scripture there is no certainty of faith, and this would be the shattering of revelation. Obviously we must conclude that the canon came into being through much struggle on the part of believers and perhaps of unbelievers, occasionally *confusione hominum* (with the confusion of men), *providentia Dei* (by divine providence). We regard the establishing of the canon in its broad content likewise as the work of the revealing Spirit, and again link it to the church fathers.[174]

e) The "Word of God" and the "Word of Man" in Scripture

Our fathers gave much reflection to the relationship between the Word of God and the word of man, and in recent times much has been written on this subject. Methodological caution makes it doubtful that one should dare to make too many statements here. Involuntarily one is reminded of the saying of the Pietists: "Something must be left for eternity." However, if one finds fault with the old doctrine of verbal inspiration, terming it a "miracle," and yet asserts the *theopneustia* (Spirit's authorship) of the Scriptures to be a "marvel," this is foolish.[175] For the vaguest form of inspiration, to the degree that it clings to "God" as the cause, is just as much a "miracle of the supernatural origin of Scripture"[176] as the most highly developed verbal inspiration, such as that of Matthias Flacius.[177]

As our orthodox fathers conceived it, if the revealing God is the principle cause (*causa principalis*) of Scripture, and human authors come into consideration only as a lesser determining cause (*causa minus principalis*), then the latter, "through inspiration of the Holy Ghost put their hand to the writing tool and at various places at various times prepared the Scriptures."[178] What was to be written depended on the influence of the Holy Spirit *(suggerebat/suggessit),* both pertaining to subject matter and pertaining to the words—in faithful continuation of the ancient church's concept and manner of expression, from Augustine to the conciliarists.[179] "Writing assistants" *(amanuenses)* or "secretaries" of the Holy Spirit is the traditional designation for the men who wrote the Bible.[180] Only in one area was there disagreement among the fathers: A majority claimed that the Hebrew vowel signs were not dependent on God as the primary cause, but on the human writers themselves.[181] The differing possible vocalization in the Hebrew text, as also all kinds of variants in the text of both the Old Testament and the New Testament, practically forced this conclusion.

Nevertheless, the defense of Matthias Flacius, who sided with the minority in this argument, lays bare the main nerve of the subject, and therefore we quote him more precisely: "If the churches permit the devil to establish this hypothesis (of the later addition of the Hebrew vowel signs), will not then all of Scripture become uncertain? But in no way should one admit that the Holy Ghost has placed before us such a dark and exceedingly inarticulately written doctrine about God, when He wanted it written just for this reason, that the doctrine could be clearly understood by the church, to show the true way to revere God and find salvation."[182] Almost prophetically Flacius anticipated that with the first break in the dam the whole dam would continue to erode. These exceptions to verbal inspiration were followed by retreats to content inspiration (only the subject matters are inspired) and to personal inspiration (only the person is inspired, but one cannot say anything very specific about the product),[183] until finally higher criticism, which became a methodological statement of faith, swept out everything else and created its own canon in the canon.

A remarkable observation can be made in this connection. The more one perceived noninspired elements in Scripture, the more it was thought one could penetrate the mysterious *event* of revelation. The solutions of content and personal inspiration, just as also the higher-critical method, are marked by the fact that scholars believed they were on the trail of more and more complicated processes as to the "how" of revelation—a point on which revelation itself is noticeably silent. The more one moves away from verbal inspiration, the more one falls into theosophical speculation.

We interject something else. Like J. A. Bengel[184] we as discerning Bible scholars must take note of the fact that in the course of several thousand years copyists' errors, gaps, variants, and different vowel signs and punctuation entered the Scriptural text. But this does not alter the fact that the Bible presents an astonishingly faithful rendition of the original text, because the variants do not change the overall context, and only seldom do they bear much weight. It does, however, place before us the task of finding the original text, and then the task of developing a methodologically appropriate concept of inspiration. In doing so, we must not skip over the above-mentioned basic concern of Matthias Flacius.

One can do justice to this basic concern if, in following revelation itself, one views *everything* that has been revealed as inspired, that is, everything we meet in Scripture which in practice claims divine inspiration. We cannot pass over the mystery of the *intermixing* of man's word with God's Word. The attempt to inquisitively unravel this intermixture and ultimately to divide it into quantitatively definable entities was the gross mistake of the higher-critical method. The comparison with the "two natures" in the Revelator, Jesus Christ, is closely related to what is divine and human in the revealed Word.[185] This means the determined and complete return to a form of verbal inspiration. It means, further, the methodological renunciation of the attempt to penetrate the "how" of the process of revelation, insofar as revelation itself does not speak of it in occasional passages. Included in this consideration are the detailed conceptions of the fathers with their carefully worded distinctions and exceptions, which we will leave undecided.[186]

f) The Problem of "Contradictions" and "Scientific Errors" and the Infallibility of Scripture

But can the tensions between Scriptural content and verbal inspiration actually be harmonized? To answer this question we must again refer back to revelation. There we see that the revealed writings, in relation to each other or within themselves, occasionally make differing statements on a subject. One need only be reminded, for example, of the genealogies of Jesus in Matthew 1 and Luke 3, or the thrice-told story of St. Paul's conversion, Acts 9, 22, and 26. Usually such variants are referred to as "contradictions." From the standpoint of today's scholarship the reproaches are further broadened to include "scientific errors," such as the often-cited Biblical reference to the rabbit as a "cud-chewing animal,"[187] or the location of hell "under the earth," or the standing-still of the sun over Gibeon,[188] and the like.

A plethora of questions now attacks not just any daring architect of the doctrine of inspiration, but even revelation itself. All accommodations in the doctrine cannot divert the attacks on revelation. When one observes this, one certainly should be very careful in sorting out the inquiries. After careful examination the "scientific errors" shrink materially: The rabbit, according to the indications used in the Old Testament, really is a "cud chewer"; with certain assumptions one certainly can speak of the "sun standing still" over Gibeon; the reference to hell as "under the

70

earth" is possible because this is a manner of expression which includes a value judgment, [189] and so forth. The problem is not created by attacks which attempt to introduce a *value judgment* different from revelation, but rather by various statements *within* revelation and the problems of the written text that has been handed down.

It would be extremely dangerous if we in this situation would attempt to become somewhat of an arbitrator between the various people who speak for God, or what is just as tempting, to become one who supposedly presents revelation better than the emissary of God who was sent for this purpose. If we had to proceed methodologically from the idea of the sovereignty of God, then also now an act of humility is the correct methodological result. That is to say, in the first place: We refrain from saying more than we can say honestly. This implies further: We must let various statements stand without offering our instructional assistance to the apostles; we must simply bear with them for the present. To be sure, we must say clearly that, in keeping with the basic rule: "Scripture must be explained by Scripture," we need to put forth the utmost effort to use our gifts so as to discover mutual agreement in Scriptural passages. The often sadistic desire to elaborate on contradictions has no support in the Biblical method. It must remain just as clear that agreement cannot be claimed beyond the methodologically responsible ability of the Bible scholar, for also therein something other than the methodologically required humility would become evident.

If now, on the one hand, the idea of the sovereignty of God associated with the concept of the entire and verbal inspiration of Scripture has been methodologically established, but on the other hand, varying statements in the texts and certain deviations in the handed-down versions can be seen, then the conclusion is inescapable that the Revelator *wants* to meet us *just in this way*. Should there actually be contradictory statements, and should we be unable to arrive at the true text [190]—which we probably never could say with complete certainty—then God would have put up with them and would have used also the "errors" as tools of His Spirit, and it would not have been the mistake of the apostles to have placed them before us. Yes, we go a step further—consciously for a moment we overstep the boundary line of speculation—and we draw out the methodological consequence to the point that even conscious errors of God's emissaries, which He does not correct but lets appear in the text, are protected by God. That is to say, we understand the "infallibility" of Scripture, of which the fathers spoke, in the sense of authorization and fulfillment by God, and not in the sense of anthropological[191] inerrancy. Insofar as textual difficulties are concerned, we also accept the continuation of divine guidance and foresight (*providentia Dei*), without indulging in the idea of progressive or unterminated revelation and without being relieved of searching for the best possible form of the text. With such assumptions we seem to remain in tune with the spiritual experience of the congregation, which, partly because of the minimal importance of the deviations and variations, confirmed the unity of the Scriptures and by its use of Scripture saw revelation fulfilling its purpose in offering salvation.

We give an example of such protection of His messenger by God, which as authority and fulfillment of His words presents an important content of inspiration according to Scripture. The example is taken from the book of the prophet Haggai, who said to Zerubbabel, the governor of Judah under the Persians: "I [the Lord] will overthrow the throne of kingdoms. . . . In that day, saith the Lord of hosts, will I take thee, O Zerubbabel, My servant, the son of Shealtiel, saith the Lord, and will make thee as a signet; for I have chosen thee, saith the Lord of hosts" (2:22-23). As all interpreters note, one could understand these words entirely in such a way that Zerubbabel should again be king in a free Judah. Perhaps Haggai himself understood the message in this way. It cannot even be completely excluded that Haggai revealed this understanding of the message and combined it with political intentions. Then, quite unobtrusively, Zerubbabel disappeared. But God did not recall His emissary. He fulfilled His own words in the history of salvation, which with and beyond Zerubbabel leads to the Offspring of David, Jesus. "There failed not ought of any good thing . . . all came to pass" (Joshua 21:45).[192] As K. H. Rengstorf explained in his excellent article on *apostello,* etc., in the *Theological Dictionary to the New Testament,*[193] one may gain understanding by referring to the Semitic rights of a messenger, according to which the messenger may directly represent his lord, as happened in the shameful treatment of David's emissaries to

King Hanun[194] or also in the case of a marriage solemnized by proxy. In a similar way the comprehensive protection, even the equality of the emissary with the one who sends him, finds expression in the answer of Jesus to Philip: "He that hath seen Me hath seen the Father" (John 14:9), or the mission statement of Jesus: "He that receiveth you receiveth Me" (Matt. 10:40).[195] Herein—and all the way into the logical consequences—we meet the secret of revelation, and not in fables about "the servant-form of revelation."

g) The Range of Inspiration

A concluding and clarifying answer is still necessary to the question: How far does inspiration extend in the individual case? In a superficial glance it would seem that also this question has been fully answered in the above explanations. But until now we have still overlooked the observation that among those who speak in Scripture, besides God and His emissaries, there are also Satan and those who speak for him; and, of course, there is man in the incomprehensible multiplicity of his being and form. It is very clear that Peter [after Jesus prophesied His own death in Jerusalem] did not appear as God's emissary when, with only Jesus and himself present, he lashed out: "Be it far from Thee, Lord; this shall not be unto Thee" (Matt. 16:22). Whereupon Jesus declared just as clearly: "Get thee behind Me, Satan, thou art an offense unto Me: for thou savourest not the things that be of God, but those that be of men" [v. 23]. We may be reminded also of Ahitophel, Judas, and above all of the false prophets, false teachers, who in the name of God acted as men of piety, saintliness, and confidence in God.[196] The Gospels are full of varying statements about Jesus. The Old Testament as well as the New Testament name not only the sins of earthly and spiritual Israel—as of course also the sins of the godless—but also those of the patriarchs, prophets, and apostles.[197] According to the revealed Word, there is only One who is "without sin."[198]

Further, there are Scripture portions that can be read and judged from various aspects. An often-cited example may be found in the imprecatory psalms of the Old Testament,[199] which we can interpret either as a human outcry and revelation of our hearts, or as a prophetic glance at the terrible wrath of God. We have a differently situated example in St. Paul's appeal to the emperor. This appeal became, on the one hand, a divine means of placing Paul "before kings" as a witness, in accordance with the prophecy in Acts 9.[200] On the other hand, the Book of Acts tells in an unembellished way that St. Paul could have been set free if he had not appealed to the emperor (Acts 26:32). Above all, in the *Ketubim* (Job, Psalms, Proverbs, Ecclesiastes, Song of Solomon) the distinction between the "human" and the "divine" is not always simple. Here the interpreter requires wisdom and restraint. Much is illuminated by the rule that Scripture interprets itself; many a particular point, however, must be left open for the present. The frequent misuse of a multiple meaning in Scripture and Luther's harping on the *sensus literalis* (literal sense)[201] should not exclude occasional multiple usage.[202] Finally, we maintain that we so interpret inspiration with regard to the human or Satanic discourse within Scripture that it tells us the truth about both, and in this form reveals to us not only the reality but also the love of God in history, which is His story.

3. Scripture and Revelation Elsewhere

a) *The Problem of Scripture and Tradition*

The inquiry here begun can be divided primarily into three areas: the problem of Scripture and tradition; the problem of Scripture and history; and finally, the problem of the relationship of Scripture to other religions. We can address each of these spheres of interest only to the extent that each has significance in forming the basis of an exegetical method. Nevertheless, it would be a mistake to leave this subject untouched, since exegetical consequences will necessarily encroach upon the interpreter, for example from the history of religion or from confessional commitment.

The problem of Scripture and tradition has been preponderantly a case of dispute between denominations and will continue to be debated by Protestant and Roman Catholic theologians as long as there exists a Roman Catholic teaching office on the one hand and a Bible-oriented Protestant church on the other. In our opinion the entire history of the origin of the Biblical canon teaches that at least the church during its formative period sought an authoritative divine norm and *separated it from its own authority.* That is to say, the problem of Scripture and tradition at that time was solved in such a way that church tradition itself determined that the divinely authorized Biblical canon must be *superior to tradition.* Whoever puts Scripture and later tradition on equal footing is acting contrary to the earlier tradition. Above all, such action is contrary to the concept of the sufficiency of Scripture, expressed in Scripture itself.

Nevertheless, the extra-Biblical and post-Biblical tradition of the church fulfills a positive function in several ways and therefore must not without further thought be made an adversary of Scripture by the interpreter. Rather, tradition is, to begin with, the bearer of the transmitted Biblical record in that it continues to hand down the texts and text variants. This means that the interpreter of today remains *dependent* on tradition in his initial and basic procedure of finding the text. Further, the sensible interpreter will not reject the help which tradition offers in understanding a text. Everything evil that one has ever said about earlier authorities cannot do away with the important fact that they stand closer than we to what is reported in the Bible—at least temporally, perhaps also spiritually. As interpreters we should again become more modest and also more careful, and not simply let modern, that is, personal critique overthrow centuries-old unanimous testimony. The ease with which certain groups in modern Protestantism do this was surely still unknown to Luther, for example.

Church tradition has, of course, not only produced doctrinal opinions, statements, and commentaries but has also issued council decrees and confessions with the intent of making them binding on everyone. If one can compare the other elements to a "caution" sign, then the latter would be a "stop" sign. To be sure, it is easy to recognize that council decrees as well as confessions argue according to Scripture, and consequently place themselves under Scripture. For while God says what is valid in Scripture, men attempt in council proceedings and confessions to render obedience to this valid truth. If we now proceed from the recognized council decrees and confessions, then it is clear at the same time that these do bear particular weight because of the momentousness of the decision and also because of the large number of those who are involved and profess their faith, who thereby seek to follow their Lord. Accordingly, it is still true that only Scripture is infallible. Councils and confessions seek to and must meet the standards of Scripture, and remain basically capable of improvement. For the interpreter, however, it must remain the rule that only after thorough study and only when Scripture offers him no other way out may he cross the boundary drawn there. For—and this again underlines the seriousness of the decision—it is the necessary responsibility of past as well as future confessions or decisions of church councils to guard against false doctrine and to establish a boundary beyond which begins a zone of spiritual death.[203]

Finally, in surveying the problem area of Scripture and tradition we are faced with the question concerning the Spirit in the church and in its tradition. It would obviously be exegetically and methodologically "unspiritual" to approach both with a somehow preconceived negative opinion. It is precisely the great promises, given to the church of the New Covenant by the Father of Jesus Christ through His Son, which permit us to see the preservation and power of the church to the present day in the light of His grace.[204] And these great promises also lead the interpreter to humble respect, which then puts the burden of proof on him when in a Scripture passage he attempts to deny the Spirit in the church. However, it is the question of certainty which ultimately drives us again and again to Scripture alone as the only refuge.

b) The Problem of Scripture and History

The second problem, that of the relationship of Scripture and history, of Scriptural revelation and historical revelation, likewise has many sides.

To begin with, God of course is active also in the history of people, and the witness of this has entered Scripture. Inasmuch as men have written the Scriptures, published them, preached them, and followed them, Scripture again constitutes a historical subject of study, indeed one that even atheists can grasp. In fact, we could establish that the revelation of Scripture occasionally follows upon revelation in history, as for example in the Gospels.

From the observation that historical processes initially are open in the sense that God's hand in history is recognizable only after a certain amount of time has elapsed,[205] some could be led to the temptation or also the pious effort to draw firm conclusions about God's action *during* the process of those historical events. Old examples of this may be found in Saul's hasty sacrifice[206] or in Shimei's curse of David.[207] Tragic modern examples are found in the movement of the "German Christians" and in the "theology of revolution."[208]

If and when history as revelation is made to mean that God is now saying something new or less or other than He said in Scripture, the interpreter would have to offer resistance on the basis of the methodological principles explained above, especially because of the authority of Scripture, in view of the purpose of Scripture to inspire confidence, and because of the sufficiency of Scripture. This is true also with regard to theological filters. If the interpretive process is to distinguish in principle between "then" and "now," that is, replace *man,* opposed to God, with *modern* man contrasted with a different type of earlier man, this would be nothing else than the silent presupposition that by virtue of the intervening history, which has brought about a change in man, God desires that another message be heard and obeyed. Such a myth about modern man the interpreter should not pursue out of Scripture. Otherwise he would look upon history as a corrective source of revelation, over against and in opposition to the Scriptures.[209]

Things are different, however, when the interpreter, conscious of his own fallibility, looks for practical objectives in his interpretation. The consciousness of fallibility here is intensified by the realization of historical restriction and limitation, e. g., in Luther's interpretation of the Antichrist as applying to the pope.[210] Something similar could be said about the pointed references to conduct, for example, in the Pharisees' fondness for titles, which Jesus castigates in Matthew 23, or in the service of mammon found in the "rich" churches. Since we are now in a time of eschatological events, which according to God's plan point to the return of Jesus, and since at the same time we are to be transformed into the image of our coming Lord in keeping with our new birth, the theologically responsible exegete will have to inquire about the significance of this for today. He will, however, do this in such a way that he will more and more let himself be influenced by Scripture and fear nothing so much as to be ranked with the deceivers who cry, "Lo, here is Christ!" or even, "I am the Christ!" For this reason he will declare the consciousness of his fallibility clearly and reject all prophetic arrogance.

c) The Relationship of Scripture to Other Religions

Also the third problem, which takes its form from the relationship of Scripture to other religions, shows up at every bend in the theological road. Beyond the special consideration of religious-historical comparison, this subject demands a basic methodological clarification for every Biblical exegesis.

The definition "other" religions can already arouse suspicion, since theologians like Karl Barth have repudiated religion as being the way of man to God; they find it opposed to the Christian faith, according to which God comes to man. Phenomenologically, on the other hand, it can hardly be disputed that Christian discipleship is "also" a religion, and in this sense we want to use that definition. Since being religious is part of being human, the Biblical exegete may and should take this phenomenon into account. Desperate a-religious statements build more barriers than bridges for understanding. In particular, understanding and comparing past as well as contemporary religions serves to clarify Biblical assertions. This is likewise true in regard to pseudoreligious philosophies and ideologies. However, the elite-like character of other philosophies or ideologies urges restraint as we approach them.

If establishing a *connection* with other religions is generally unobjectionable, the situation changes when we pass from explanation to the area of obligation. If we take seriously the authority of Scripture as developed above, then every attempt at making Scripture relative in relation to other religions is likewise plainly forbidden. One sets aside both the purpose of Scripture and the certainty of faith by dealing with Biblical statements as though they were truisms "among others." At this point the difference between the general historical method and the historical-Biblical method again finds expression. As little as one can add history to Scripture as a dependable source of revelation, so little can one add another religion to serve as such.

This recognition, to begin with, precludes using a non-Biblical religious statement to establish the correctness of a Biblical one. Reference to the *consensus gentium*,[211] which Kant, for example, used in his argumentation, can be very helpful in making missionary *contacts,* but it is not genuine theological *proof.* At the same time this makes it clear that, when it comes to establishing the meaning of a Biblical statement, it does not suffice to quote a similar statement from the history of religion, under the tacit or expressed supposition that the Bible means exactly the same as what is stated in that source.

Moreover, a dialog in the classic Greek sense, which makes it possible to discover truth through mutual exchange of opinions, is out of the question in Biblical exegesis. Dialog, however, which clarifies positions, indicates points of contact, and tries to understand them is not excluded.

The question as to the extent to which God's Holy Spirit offers truth also to other religions we can answer only with restraint. Certainly a Biblical statement is not less dependable just because a like or similar one is also found elsewhere. Devaluation because of similarities in the history of religion would be just as much a mistake as increasing value because of such similarities. On the other hand, the merely "religious" person finds himself in a curious "in between" state. God as his Creator supports and protects him also as far as his intellectual life is concerned. At the same time, according to Romans 1, he is given up by God because of his sin, especially with reference to his knowledge of God (Rom. 1:18 ff.); according to Romans 2 he is spiritually blind; and according to Romans 3 he is without exception guilty. In no case do the other religions offer a revelation that makes for certainty, and therefore they offer nothing to supplement Scripture.

To what has been said we must, however, note another exception: Israel according to the flesh. We cannot simply classify Judaism with "other religions." For "the covenant and the promises" still belong to it (Rom. 9:4). The authority of the Scriptures of the Old Testament is also its divine authority and life-giving basis. To that degree its fathers are our fathers. For that reason it will be able to give a particular contribution to the understanding of the Old Testament and, to be sure in a different manner, also of the New Testament. Certainly there remains for the present the "veil" over Judaism's knowledge of Scripture, "which . . . is done away in Christ" (2 Cor. 3:14 ff.). Therefore we must not put the lordship and gift of the Christ on the same level in the Old Covenant as we find them revealed in the New.

In summary, we have established that every exegesis must be based on Scripture. There is no certainty outside of Scripture.

4. Procedural Steps of the Historical-Biblical Method

a) Preliminary Remarks

Also here we are aware that this is merely an exploratory presentation. We would be well advised to take careful note of what useful insights the historical-critical method offered. Even where its conclusions led to error, it made many good observations. As in other fields, there were highly gifted scholars with eminent talents, distinguished also by their diligence, precision, and devotion to their work. To deny all this would be foolish. While we thankfully accept what is good, our human regard for their accomplishments and our esteem for those whom we came to know as teachers should not obstruct the path to right conclusions concerning the Bible. In what follows it should also be noted that the Biblical method does not consist simply of the listed individual steps but that these must be viewed as a whole from the standpoint of the previously outlined basic considerations. When one seeks to understand the differences, these often strike a person not so much in the details as in the context of the total view.

b) Finding the Text

For all scholarly work with the Scriptures, the first responsibility is that of finding the text. There are literally countless variants, and the number is constantly increasing, for example through the collecting of ancient lectionaries. The comparison of variants must be carried out critically, that is, with reasonable and intelligent standards. The term "textual criticism," to be sure, leaves room for misunderstanding, for it does not infer criticism of the text but refers to critically *finding* the text out of a choice that sometimes is very limited and at other times quite extensive. Nevertheless, also this task remains subject to general theological and methodological principles and is therefore clearly an aspect of theology. Methodologically speaking, the insight is important that a result must be reached from various considerations. For example, the more difficult reading *(lectio difficilior)*, which generally is given precedence, could possibly be the result of a scribal error and therefore have little meaning. Besides this, especially the theologian should guard against falling prey to a good-manuscripts myth and therefore following in blind confidence whenever certain manuscripts provide certain readings. A third warning concerns the procedure which follows the axiom that the longer version indicates a later refinement. As a matter of fact, in later times people were not adverse to abridging, and especially the hard-working copyist was more inclined to leave something out than to add to the text.

c) Translation

After the text has been established, we must translate it as exactly and as pointedly as possible. Every inclination to neglect the Biblical languages (Hebrew, Aramaic, Greek, and because of old translations also Latin) should be met with determined resistance. Such knowledge of languages is becoming ever more necessary, since translations and paraphrases of Biblical texts continue to abound with bewildering profusion. Thorough and diligent philological work is indispensable. At the same time, theology must pursue its own language study, for language developments which are of interest to theology are not of equal interest to general linguistic study. This is true, for example, for the Greek used in Judaism, which colored Biblical translation with characteristic "Semitisms" (peculiarities taken from the Semitic languages). This is true also for oriental Greek, as used for example in Egypt, for the Greek of the common people (the so-called Koine), and the language of religious literature at the time the Bible was written, as also the language of administration and of private societies, etc. The translator will again and again encounter concepts which can be interpreted differently, depending on their origin and area of usage. It is obvious that one must interpret by taking other parts of Scripture into consideration— for example, clarifying New Testament concepts from Old Testament passages. Here again the methodological principle is verified: "Scripture interprets itself" *(Scriptura sui ipsius interpres).*

d) The Contemporary Historical Background

Our next procedural step is that of illuminating the contemporary historical background. Exegesis must discard all fear of history. Here the fact that the method has a justifiable historical interest is documented. Clearly and humbly the method must indeed recognize that correct interpretation, with salvation in view, does not presuppose a knowledge of contemporary history, or any historical instruction at all. However, false interpretation can more readily be avoided by giving consideration to historical circumstances. The advantage of sincere scholarly activity here becomes very evident. For example, if we are looking at the incident of the "tribute money" (Matt. 22:15 ff.) against the background of contemporary political movements, it becomes much clearer how Jesus set Himself apart from revolutionary Jewish zealotry and rejected improper politicizing. A comparison with socially active groups in the Roman Empire can better bring out the distinctive elements of the Christian diaconate, to mention another instance.

The exegete must draw from a wide range of historical observations. He is perhaps less concerned with the religious history of literature or with the history of philosophical ideas—to which modern Protestantism has been magically and mightily drawn—than with the highlights of daily life in those times, for example, with the material brought to light so powerfully in the parables of Jesus. It is urgently necessary to catch up with the Anglo-Saxon advances in this field. Archaeology—all the way to numismatics—claims burning theological interest.[212] The education of future theologians for this type of investigation in the past is a chapter which is best passed over. Papyri of the ancient everyday world, novels of that time, their dramas,[213] and of course the factual records of geographical, business, and political activities of that time should be available to theological scholarship. Not least, from the concept of the inspiration of Scripture and its authority in general, we must deduce the exegetical conclusion that we must everywhere take Scripture with new seriousness as a witness of history.

e) Historicoreligious Comparison

Strictly speaking, historicoreligious comparison is only a segment of the historical endeavors of our exegetical method. Just because it is that, we may not overlook it, even though the studies and results of the historicoreligious school may occasionally have brought forth some shocking things, such as the "Bible-Babel" controversy or the claim that Jesus was an Essene, among other things. As previously explained, it remains standard procedure for a Biblical methodology to concern itself with divine revelation exclusively within Scripture.[214] However, it does make for historical and theological clarification if we compare other religions with it. To this we must add two additional remarks.

In the first place, it would be a gross misunderstanding if one were to look upon historicoreligious endeavors as only condemnatory apologetics.[215] As clear as it is that only Scripture possesses divine authority, just so conscious must the interpreter be that religion as such gives expression to something generally human and that he as a human being likewise has a part in it. So the more he listens to other (contemporary) religions surrounding Scripture, the more clear the Word of God will become to him.

Second, it should not scare us if similarities to Biblical statements emerge out of the history of religion. They neither shatter and dependability of Scripture as God's Word, nor do they confirm its correctness; rather, they are part of the mystery of God's preservation of man and His abandonment of him after the fall into sin.[216] Moreover, theological importance warrants that we dedicate a specific procedural step in methodology to historicoreligious comparison.

f) Concerning Previous Literary Criticism and Form Criticism

In the area of literary criticism and form criticism, to both of which we want to address ouselves at the same time, we will note a vast difference between a historical-Biblical methodology and the historical-critical. The mere fact that the text now given to us and actually placed into our hands is the compelling norm is already sufficient reason for this. The question Marxsen asked, for example, whether we should select the first, the second, or even the third draft of a redacted Biblical document as our subject for exegetical study,[217] loses theological interest. Only impulses of erroneous curiosity, which like "the angels desire to look into" (1 Peter 1:12) the mystery of how God's revelation came into being and grew, could with constantly changing conjectures but with ever the same fallibility and fruitlessness wish to intrude upon this "theological development" of Scripture.

However, two exceptions to this must be made. The first concerns the possibility of research which seeks to explore the history of the earliest congregation by examining certain literary sources or forms, such as hymns, prayers, and the like. This can be profitable for church history, and also for exegesis, as long as the attempt does not lose sight of scholarly caution and discipline. The second exception may be seen in those cases where the concern of a text can be better understood by a knowledge of form, for example, in interpreting the parables. Here special attention must be paid to ensure that no extra-Biblical ideas or examples might force the Biblical Word into a Procrustean bed. In other words, this investigation should, first of all, be basically inner-Biblical and should be Biblically substantiated. In order to avoid erroneous results, it seems best to take this formal investigation into the other procedural steps of Biblical classification and analysis so that we can consider its points of view by comparing them with the contemporary historical background and with the history of religion.

g) Biblical Classification

What until now the historical-critical method did only in a limited way and with hesitation, will be a comprehensive necessity for the historical-Biblical method, namely, Biblical classification. It is not merely a matter of looking at the broader context of which the segment of text to be interpreted presents a part, nor of taking into consideration Biblical material under the catchword "historicoreligious comparison." Rather, the following aspects are important.

The Scriptures show us various *epochs* in the history of God's dealings with man *(Heilsgeschichte),* which Bengel paraphrases with the concepts *ordo temporum* (classification of time) and *oeconomia divina* (divine economy).[218] Bengel's theory of time, the details of which cannot be discussed here, is based on the very Scriptural statements [219] which constrained also the Reformers to discriminate between Moses and Christ, between the book of the Law and the book of grace (Luther),[220] and to discriminate between various administrations (economies, Calvin).[221] If Adam and Eve, with only one exception, were permitted to do anything they wanted, then by the time of Noah man already faced a catalog of laws. The laws and the worship at the time of the partriarchs by no means coincide with the regulations of the old covenant of Mount Sinai. Every Sunday is proof of the difference which exists between the new covenant of Golgotha and the old covenant. The millennial kingdom will again differ from the completed realm of the eternal Sabbath. The interpreter must carefully see these economies both in their unity, through the plan of the God who moves forward in them—this was a particular interest of Calvin [222]—and also in their differentiation. Church history teaches us that the fanatics *(Schwaermer)* and false teachers did away with just these differences. This may be seen, for example, in Luther's conflict with the religious rabble-rousers who fell back on Moses—as also in many of the so-called theologians of revolution, who base their arguments primarily on Old Testament prophetic texts.[223]

When the interpreter has completed the classification into the history of salvation *(Heilsgeschichte)* and taken note of the special conditions of the epoch to which the text belongs, he should then *examine parallel passages* from the entire Scriptures. In comparing a number of statements from various epochs, a specific, uniform concern, a *typical* one, can often be brought out in and through historical considerations. Such a procedure has nothing in common with that often denounced "fragmentation method" of the *dicta probantia,*[224] but rather is called forth by the "Scripture interprets itself" rule, especially by the way the New Testament makes use of the Old. We mentioned previously how Jesus in the Book of Jonah on the one hand read about the actual fate of an Old Testament prophet but on the other hand saw in it the prototype of His own destiny. Just so the Letter to the Hebrews sees past reality in the Old Testament and at the same time sees in it the "image" and the "shadow" of what is to come.[225] Finally, also St. Paul says that in the Old Testament there was the "shadow of things to come" and is of the opinion that what is written there was experienced "typically" *(typicos)* by the people then and has been preserved in the Holy Scriptures for our warning or perception.[226] The unity and unfolding of Scripture will establish their own validity in this manner. Both the dynamics of Scripture and the praise-demanding insight into a part of God's plan are then imparted to the interpreter. By means of this praise the interpreter establishes fellowship with the worshiping congregation, into which St. Paul, e.g. in Rom. 11:33 ff., rightly incorporates us.

We want to add to what has just been said, emphasizing one particular aspect. In accordance with God's plan, Scripture is a book with a purpose, and not just a simple book of revelation for the curious, even as it is not a book of divine chit-chat. Its purpose is the salvation of him to whom it speaks, the reading and listening individual.[227] It seeks to rescue this individual from the coming judgment of God and to make him a member of God's eternal kingdom. Therefore it is aimed toward the future, both for the individual and for the community. In this sense, by virtue of its continuity from the first to the last page, which again takes up the first page, it is *eschatologically oriented.* It is the responsibility of the interpreter, in conformity with the Scriptures, to construe Scripture not only historically but truly eschatologically-apocalyptically. Whoever overlooks this Biblical continuity brings the text he is interpreting into fatal isolation.

h) The Analysis

After the procedural steps previously touched upon, the exegete can undertake a thorough and balanced analysis, faithful to the context. The goal of the analysis is to present a total view of what has been gained from the previous procedural steps, and it logically culminates in one or more sentences that summarize the primary content and scope of the text. Where the importance or the peculiarity of a given text requires a more thorough investigation, which might thus far not have been done, this must take the form of a separate little treatise [228] immediately preceding the analysis. When we speak of a "balanced" analysis we do not mean that painful theological striving for playing it safe all around, where one sentence is dialectically balanced with another and theological initiative and theological clarity are ultimately the losers. We mean, rather, the methodologically conscious, disciplined, and if possible complete application of what has been worked out. Stuhlmacher indicates this is his fourth thesis when he states: "Biblical texts are interpreted in a historically adequate way only when they are examined with the help of a controlled synthesis of the various individual methods, mutually correcting one another."[229]

The analysis should take a theological position. This sentence must be clarified from two points of view. Taking a position, to begin with, assumes that one is conversant with secondary literature. Included in this is patristic and Reformation literature, along with the writings of the moderns. As much as the interpreter should be led into theological questions and struggles by the other voices, just so selective should he be when it comes to setting up hypotheses. "The present . . . propensity for chaotically formulating hypotheses in the exegetical field" is justifiably criticized by level-headed interpreters with increasing frequency.[230] Also, it is not at all certain whether the widest possible use of secondary literature is a guarantee for the depth and penetrating power of a theological analysis. But then, after his responsible scholarly dialog with secondary literature, the interpreter should not shrink back from making his own clear decision. The dry or ironical reporting of what others have said will not suffice. And taking one's stance on the side of a big name is proper only if it is grounded on one's modesty. Better would be a persuasive delineation of the insights granted to the interpreter, whereby he certainly may "ride in the same carriage with learned men" as the Swabian saying has it.

After all, an analysis becomes theological only when the interpreter gives expression to *what God here wants to say to all men*. Too long have certain commentaries been content to trace the origin of a text, relying on conjectures, and then to add comparative passages from the history of religion. Perhaps they even added what "Matthew" or "John" or "Paul" wanted to say to their readers at that time. And they just did not know what kind of a breakneck venture it was to take a reconstructed picture, whose frame was filled with conjectures, and try to make a living speaker out of it—a speaker whose part in the delivered message was not even certain and whose purpose therefore remained just as much in

87

the dark as did his audience, likewise fashioned by many conjectures. We do not want to deny that even under these circumstances something worthwhile and true was left over, even though Stuhlmacher, looking at literary criticism, pronounces this bitter sentence: "Strands of sources and fragments of tradition in widest variety are probed without their origin and transmission ever being raised to the level of a historical problem."[231] But before all historical reconstructions and conjectures we must grasp the *theologein* (God speaking or God being spoken of). Further, in our analysis we should remove the veil created by the myth of the different, modern man, which through the difference brought about by history wanted to create a new recipient and therefore a new message, thus separating the historical from the theological interpretation. Such a procedure does not imply refusal to make distinctions which Scripture itself makes or confirms in various situations. But it does mean that the interpreter will refuse to make arbitrary distinctions in Biblical truth, led by his picture of "then" and "now." Rather, we find ourselves in agreement with Scripture—and thereby on the real "theological" basis—when we proceed on the foundation of the Pauline sentence: "Now all these things (really) happened unto them (those who lived in earlier times) . . . and they are written (behind the passive voice is God, who caused the writing) for our admonition, upon whom the ends of the world are come" (1 Cor. 10:11).

5. The Context and the Whole of Scripture

a) General Statements

The exegete cannot always interpret only individual passages of Scripture. As a methodizer who makes use of the historical-Biblical method he can do this even less than the historical-critical exegete, who cripples the total meaning of Scripture with his false critical analysis, sets the individual parts against each other by distinguishing wrongly between them, and finally rests content with the "blocks" he presents as reliable norms. Rather, every interpreter establishes for himself a more or less conscious total impression of Scripture, which in this or that manner usually comes through when he interprets individual portions. Since he gives himself over to reflection, this total impression necessarily develops into a theological pattern of classification. The interpretation of individual passages is brought into line with this overall pattern or occasionally perhaps also changes it.

It was our objective in this third chapter to let divine revelation, to which our interpretive efforts are being directed, determine and define itself so far as possible, and to develop our methodology accordingly. Apropos of this, we have on the basis of thorough reflection presented a conception of Scripture and of Scriptural interpretation that is in keeping with definite methodological insights.

However, it should be clear to us that in spite of the Scriptural conception and interpretation we have discussed, the Scriptures contain such an abundance of truth and such dynamics that the individual theologian will not be able to function without some kind of a personal order of priorities. In accordance with it he determines what is to be accented and stressed, and thus he will again and again be led to similar insights. Such an order of priorities is therefore absolutely necessary. To be sure, it is just at this point our responsibility to be constantly mindful of the subjectivity of the proceedings. Therefore we cannot compel others to accept what *to us* seems to be the cardinal point. While the statements of Scripture are imperishable, the theological systems we devise are all too quickly buried with us in the grave. This is our biographical sphere of activity, and we often have reason to discover the dependence of theology on biography. Biography, in turn, leads into the secret of the guidance of our life and the various gifts of the children of God.[232]

b) Three Basic Observations: The Purpose of Scripture, The History of Salvation, and the Position of Christ

With the above reservation—yes, in spite of it—we venture to suggest lines of thought which a theology based on the authority of the entire canonical Scriptures will meet again and again.

First, Scripture of the Old and New Testaments is not a purposeless book. Its primary purpose throughout is to deliver man from evil and ultimately to lead him into fellowship with God. Whatever does not serve this purpose, whether word or thought, is excluded by Scripture itself. Its content is the most necessary extract; from the point of view just mentioned, everything in it demands attention. For this reason there is a seeming lack, which invites human speculation. For this reason, too, from the first page to the last, there is a conflict on behalf of man which concerns itself with either his eternal bliss or eternal condemnation. The indolent heart of the indifferent and foolish; man's unreasonableness, which does not see what is most important; false doctrine, which leads into darkness instead of into light and into death instead of into life—all these are attacked with unparalleled severity. Where truth is at stake, Scripture knows no tolerance. It has "tolerance" only where God's patience still wants to make conversion possible or persevering love endures.[233] Unyieldingly Scripture destroys claims of revelation elsewhere. It adheres to the one way that alone has the promise of salvation.[234] One may say that for this reason it exhibits dualistic characteristics, but not dualism[235] in the sense that two forces, each with its own will, could come forward with basically equal rights. For among the "sons of God" Satan, in bondage to sin, is made a slave of God, subdued only by the Word of Christ and irrevocably condemned.

It becomes clear to the interpreter that an immensely heavy responsibility rests on him, since he himself with his activity becomes a factor in this struggle which concerns himself and other people. The Biblical interpreter is just the opposite of the "neutral scientist."

Second, Scripture bears witness to and effects salvation history *(Heilsgeschichte),* or however one may want to designate the content exactly. In contrast to human designs and deeds, it concerns the "great deeds of God" in a history whose dimensions cannot be determined by boundaries, however reliable, that mark man's world.[236] What about these acts of God? To offer no opinion on supernatural persons and events would be theological blasphemy. Scripture leaves no doubt concerning the one living God in three Persons, to whom belongs the first and the last word, whose creative power makes possible, encompasses, and forms or allows the forming of all existing things. How could we be His image if He were not a Person?

This active God, who seems most incomprehensible just in His Personhood and in His ability to become man, fits all events into His plan. That He does not do this through amechanical cause-and-effect procedure but with free powers of His will is just what incites the praise of the beholder. Because God has a plan, history has a goal. His objective in history is the salvatin of all who will accept Him. This salvation, however, presupposes the conquest and vigilant rejection of the Evil One and of everything evil that follows him. Love without righteousness is out of place. How God's love is ever new beginnings in empathetic compassion, in unswerving faithfulness amidst human perfidy, in superior victory from epoch to epoch, and finally through the end time strides to His goal and brings redeemed man with Him—that, according to Scripture, is the content of the history of salvation. Whoever does not expect the return of Jesus, whoever does not recognize the drama of choosing Him to be at his side in life, such a person according to Scripture lives "ahistorically" (unhistorically)

This active God, who seems most incomprehensible just in His Personhood and in His ability to become man, fits all events into His plan. That He does not do this through a mechanical cause-and-effect procedure but with free powers of His will is just what incites the praise of the beholder. Because God has a plan, history has a goal. His objective in history is the salvation of all who will accept Him. This salvation, however, presupposes the conquest and vigilant rejection of the Evil One and of everything evil that follows him. Love without righteousness is out of place. How God's love in ever new beginnings, in empathetic compassion, in unswerving faithfulness amidst human perfidy, in superior victory from epoch to epoch, and finally through the end time strides to His goal and brings redeemed man with Him—that, according to Scripture, is the content of the history of salvation. Whoever does not expect the return of Jesus, whoever does not recognize the drama of choosing Him to be at his side in life, such a person according to Scripture lives "ahistorically" (unhistorically) in the most profound sense.

Finally, in the third place: Every interpreter arrives at a center of Scripture which brings him joy. We have looked not only at Luther's "what teaches Christ" but also at the justification of the ungodly. There is in Scripture a turning point which cannot be overlooked, which stamps everything plainly as either "before" or "after." It is the beginning of the New Testament with Jesus, the Christ (Messiah). He was active even before His birth by Mary, for "all things were created by Him and for Him."[237]

But the fulfillment of great promises and the approaching fulfillment of all the rest, the one and final redemption, the beginning of the end-period of time before His return, and the completion of the eons—all that happened through His journey to the cross and out of the grave. Thus we can designate Christ as the middle of Scripture and its pivotal point, its center, its heart. No matter how we determine details of this central element, it always takes place in connection with Christ. But as theologians we should not be so foolish as to oppose the "center" by means of an "edge," or presumptuously to designate "peripheral zones,"[238] almost as though there were adiaphora (unimportant things) in the Scriptures. Is the skin unimportant because it constitutes the most exterior part of the body? Or could one lightheartedly lop off the point of a toe because it is located farthest from the heart? In a similar way the theologian strikes at his own center when he despises whatever is governed by it. Also there he should apply the Pauline sentence: "Those members of the body which seem to be more feeble are necessary; and those members of the body which we think to be less honorable, upon these we bestow more abundant honor . . ." (1 Cor. 12:22-23). The more value we attach to the entire Scriptures, the more glorious will He become who gave them to us and completely embodies them in Himself:

Jesus, the Christ!

NOTES

Note: Throughout the German text the author used abbreviations for the sources of his quotations, if possible only the name of the author. These abbreviations are listed in a separate line at the end of each entry in the bibliography which follows the footnote section. The translator has followed the same pattern, using the same abbreviations. Note also that here and there the translator has added information in the footnotes. This is indicated by brackets.

1. Semler, pp. 13 f., 46 f.; cf. Kuemmel, pp. 74 and 80 f. [Johann Salomo Semler (1725—91) was the "father of modern Biblical criticism," a professor of theology at the University of Halle.] His book was written 1771—76.

2. E. g., Troeltsch, *Lage,* pp. 8 ff.; Zahrndt, pp. 157 ff.

3. Cf. Stuhlmacher, *Thesen;* Hahn, pp. 1 f., 12; and Stuhlmacher, *Hermeneutik,* pp. 121, 123.

4. Joachim a Fiore (1132—1202), abbott of a Cistercian monastery in Corezzo, southern Italy, developed a peculiar doctrine of eschatology. [He prophesied a new "Age of the Spirit" in which the hierarchy of the church would be unnecessary and Christians would unite with infidels.]

5. Troeltsch, *Lage,* p. 36; Bultmann in *Kerygma und Mythos,* I, 15 ff.

6. Kaesemann, I, 194, as a modern example of this position which Troeltsch thus expressed in *Methode,* p. 735: "Whether this historicizing . . . should be seen as a blessing, that is here not the question. . . . In any event, we can no longer think without and against this method."

7. Cf. Feghelm, pp. 16 ff.; Stuhlmacher, *Hermeneutik,* pp. 123 ff.

8. Cf. Falckenberg, pp. 172 ff. and 234 ff.

9. "The fine and good man" and "man as the measure of all things."

10. "The weight of sin."

11. *Kanon,* p. 52; Semler, pp. 43, 47, 55, 58 ff.; cf. Kuemmel, p. 74, and Weber, *Schriftforschung,* p. 9.

12. *Kanon,* p. 407.

13. For this dissimilarity just compare Stuhlmacher's verdict in *Thesen,* p. 21.

14. Troeltsch, *Lage,* pp. 8 f., 36 ff.; somewhat weaker in Weber, *Schriftforschung,* pp. 31 ff., 45 ff.

15. Cf. Weber, *Schriftforschung,* pp. 167 ff.
16. *Kanon,* pp. 276, 396 ff.
17. Ibid., pp. 94 ff., 246.
18. Ibid., p. 228.
19. Ibid., pp. 53 f.
20. Lessing, p. 34. [Gotthold Ephraim Lessing, 1729—81, poet, dramatist, philosopher, and first German literary critic, was an outstanding figure in the Enlightenment. Although the son of a Lutheran pastor, he delighted in ridiculing orthodox Christianity.]
21. "Primary": original; "secondary": later.
22. *Kanon,* p. 369.
23. So Marxsen in *Kanon,* p. 246.
24. *Kanon,* p. 245.
25. Ibid., p. 94.
26. Ibid., p. 228.
27. Ibid., p. 61; "doctrinal-juridical": didactic-legal.
28. Ibid., p. 333.
29. Ibid., p. 340.
30. E. g., 1 Cor. 7:25 and vv. 10, 12.
31. Matt. 5:22, 28, 32, 34, 39, 44.
32. *Kanon,* pp. 371, 407 f.
33. "Option": free choice.
34. *Kanon,* pp. 190 ff.
35. Cf. *Kanon,* p. 192, the continuation of Kueng's train of thought; also Weber, *Schriftforschung,* pp. 45 ff.
36. Bartsch, ed., *Kerygma und Mythos,* I, 15 ff.
37. Previously there were only the so-called "cases": Jatho, F. Delitzsch with the Bible-Babel controversy, etc.
38. *Ereignisse und Gestalten,* 1878—1918, pp. 168 f.
39. Barth, p. 66, cf. p. 161.
40. Cf. Bultmann, *Theologie,* pp. 26 ff., and *Tradition,* pp. 316 ff.
41. 1 John 4:8, 16, 18.
42. *Kirchlich-Theologische-Arbeitsgemeinschaft.* [Literally translated: "Ecclesiastical-Theological Work-Fellowship." The German text uses only the abbreviation "KTA" because these groups are well known in Germany. Since the name as such means little to those outside of Germany, it has been translated simply as "church study groups."]
43. The differences between the Protestant and Roman Catholic conceptions, for example in regard to the Apocryphal Books, need not be considered at this stage of our discussion.
44. Known in English as *On the Bondage of the Will.* [This is one of Luther's most profound treatises, written in his literary battle with Erasmus. Luther held

that the unconverted man is in bondage, a slave of sin, until he is made free through God's grace.]

45. Pascal, p. 15.

46. A false teacher ca. A.D. 150.[In attempting to free Christianity from Jewish influence he rejected all of the Old Testament and much of the New.]

47. Cf. Joest's thesis, p. 151: "The primary command remains for it (theology) to do what it must do with regard to *its* subject and its responsibility." See also the early insight concerning the *method* in Weber, *Schriftforschung*, p. 45: "What is the method? A glance at the crisis lets it become a problem," as also the judgment of Troeltsch, *Methode*, p. 734: "The determining factor is the verification and productiveness of a method."

48. Nevertheless, Kueng and Lengsfeld, who are the two Roman Catholics, are by no means figureheads or alibi pleaders, but stand for the ecumenical open-mindedness and the general principles of all the essays in this volume. To avoid misunderstandings, this should be specifically noted.

49. Cf. Hahn's statement, p. 3: "It should not be contested that we find ourselves at the end of, or at least in a late phase of, a process of disintegration which has been in progress for several centuries."

50. We are omitting several authors (Gloege, Cullmann, Lengsfeld), not disparagingly, but solely because in our opinion they would *here* contribute nothing essentially new or supplementary to our subject.

51. *Kanon,* pp. 60 f.

52. Bornkamm, p. 177.

53. Ibid., p. 179.

54. Ibid., p. 178: "Some good pious man . . .who took up a number of statements by the understudies of the apostles and threw everything together on paper, or perhaps it is taken from a sermon written by another person."

55. Ibid., p. 179.

56. Luther insisted on a doctrine of the real presence of the body and blood of Christ in the Sacrament, whereas Zwingli taught a *representation* concept.

57. Quoted from the Munich Edition of *Luther's Works,* I, 15.

58. Bornkamm, p. 177.

59. Ibid., p. 175.

60. Literally translated: "spoken against, questioned by some." [These are certain New Testament books about whose canonicity there was some uncertainty in the early church. They are James, Jude, 2 and 3 John, 2 Peter, Hebrews, and the Apocalypse.—*Lutheran Cyclopedia,* p. 37.]

61. "Forensic" in the sense of a legal process.

62. Now in Kaesemann, II, 69 ff.

63. Cf. Matt. 5—7, Luke 6, Matt. 15; from Qumran especially the Habakkuk commentary.

64. Cf. 1 Cor. 9:21; John 15; Gal. 6:2; Rom. 13:10.

65. E. g. in 2 Cor. 5:10 and in the Son of Man words.

66. Both words mean "doctrine."

67. 1 and 2 Timothy and Titus.

68. In this connection Kaesemann rightly complains: "In the Protestant debate on the problem of the canon, the element of doctrine in the New Testament fell short" (*Kanon,* p. 399).

69. *Kanon,* p. 340.

70. Ibid., p. 189.

71. Bornkamm, p. 177.

72. *Kanon,* p. 41.

73. Ibid., pp. 92 ff.; "Logos" means Word (of God), [synonym for Christ in John 1].

74. That is, Luther's formula: "What teaches or deals with Christ."

75. On this specific point cf. Ph. Vielhauer, "Gottesreich und Menschensohn in der Verkuendigung Jesu," Festschrift in honor of Guenther Dehn, Neukirchen, 1967, pp. 51 ff.

76. Representatives of "form criticism" are Bultmann, Dibelius, and K. L. Schmidt.

77. Naturally various interpretations of a personal type could have resulted, which, however, proceeded from what had actually been said prior to interpretation.

78. "Factual": the actual, received canon.

79. Christology: the doctrine that treats the Person of Christ. Anthropology: the study of man.

80. *Kanon,* pp. 223 and 228 f. respectively.

81. "Man as the measure of all things."

82. *Kanon,* p. 383.

83. Especially, e. g., Kaesemann, *Kanon,* pp. 383 ff.

84. *Kanon,* pp. 245 f.

85. Kaesemann, I, 194.

86. Even though, self-evidently, a difference can exist between "Old Testament" and "Jewish."

87. First appeared in *Evangelische Theologie,* 11, 1951/52, pp. 13 ff.

88. Cf. *Kanon,* pp. 371, 407.

89. Ibid., pp. 407 f.

90. Ibid., pp. 370 f.; cf. pp. 190, 351.

91. Ibid., pp. 371 and 402 respectively; cf. p. 131.

92. Ibid., p. 376.

93. Ibid., p. 405; cf. pp. 403 f., 407.

94. Ibid., p. 369.

95. Kaesemann in *Kanon,* pp. 368 f.

96. Cf. [Gerhard Kittel, ed.], *Theologisches Woerterbuch* [*Theological Dictionary*], VII, 966 ff.

97. "Medicine of immortality."

98. Kaesemann, II, 100, 130.

99. *Kanon,* p. 189.

100. "Self-evidence" in the sense of "proving itself."

101. *Kanon,* pp. 173 f.; cf. also p. 167.

102. Cf. Kaesemann's comments in *Kanon,* pp. 362 ff.

103. "Contingent": historically coming into existence through special circumstances. "Complex": consisting of many elements.

104. *Kanon,* pp. 253 ff.

105. Ibid., p. 280; cf. pp. 261, 275.

106. Ibid., pp. 275 f.

107. Ibid., p. 276; cf. Kaesemann's comments, pp. 396 ff.

108. Ibid., pp. 297 and 330 respectively

109. Ibid., pp. 330 f.

110. Ibid., p. 333.

111. Ibid., pp. 189 ff.

112. Ibid., p. 192.

113. Ibid., p. 198. *Complexio oppositorum:* something made up of opposites.

114. Ecclesiology: the doctrine of the church. Soteriology: the doctrine of salvation. Christology: the doctrine of Christ. See footnote 79.

115. *Kanon,* pp. 155 ff.

116. Ibid., p. 123.

117. Hirsch, *Hilfsbuch,* pp. 317 ff.

118. Ps. 119:133.

119. Docetism: A heretical doctrine found in connection with various sects in the early Christian era who taught that Christ only *seemed* to be a human being, but had not really come in the flesh. Therefore the One crucified only seemed to be human.

120. In recent times, e.g., Feghelm, Hahn, Hengel, Stuhlmacher.

121. Even among secular historiographers there are changes and conflict about method. One need think only of such divergent historians as Ranke, Spengler, or Toynbee, or even those caught up in Marxism.

122. Cf. Hengel, pp. 84 f.; Joest, pp. 150 f.; Kuemmel, pp. 80 f.; Troeltsch, *Lage,* pp. 36 ff.; Weber, *Schriftforschung,* pp. 6, 31, 58 ff. Troeltsch still spoke of the "omnipotence of analogy"; cf. his *Methode,* p. 732.

123. At Cannae, in SE Italy, Hannibal defeated the Romans in 216 B.C. [The Caudine Forks are narrow passes in the Apennines in southern Italy, where in 321 B.C. the Samnites routed a Roman army and forced it to pass under a yoke.—*Columbia Cyclopedia,* 3rd ed., 1963, p. 364.]

124. Again cf. Hengel, pp. 84 f.

125. We are avoiding the concept "historical-theological," which, for example, is used again in Stuhlmacher, *Thesen,* p. 20—and Hengel's theses also suggest—because the rest of theology in its authoritative quality differs from the Bible, and "historical-theological," would lead us beyond the Bible.

126. The well-known *ubi et quandum visum est Deo,* Augsburg Confession, V.

127. Joest, pp. 150 f., here states correctly: "It cannot be the primary commandment for theology to firmly integrate itself with a general concept of scholarship and then observe what it, under threat of punishment for becoming 'unscholarly' may or may not do in relation to its particular subject and its particular responsibility."

128. Cf. H. A. Oberman's book; also Boehmer, *Luther,* pp. 122 f.; also Boehmer, *Forschung,* p. 48.

129. John 3:1 ff.

130. Among numberless references, cf. Ex. 3:14; 6:2 ff.; Deut. 32:39; 1 Sam. 3:7; Ps. 46:11; Is. 41:4; 43:11 ff.; 45:5; Matt. 11:25 ff.; John 14:21; 17:6; Rom. 3:21; 9:14 ff.; 1 Cor. 2:10; 2 Cor. 2:14; 1 Tim. 3:16; 2 Tim. 1:10; 1 Peter 1:12.

131. For the attempts to reach certainty, cf. Stuhlmacher's second thesis and Hengel, p. 87.

132. Weimar Edition, VII, 96 ff., quoted in Hirsch, *Hilfsbuch,* p. 85.

133. Cf. Luther, *idem:* Scripture aims at "condeming the wrongness of our effort, calling us back to the source, and teaching that first and only should one concentrate on God's Word; but may the Spirit of His own free will come and drive out our spirit so that we may be theologians without danger." See also the continuation. Cf. also Stuhlmacher's crushing judgment concerning the custom of occupying oneself chiefly with secondary literature (*Thesen,* pp. 18 f.).

134. Among recent statements, cf. Hengel, p. 9 (very restrained), and Stuhlmacher's *Thesen,* p. 20.

135. Characteristic is here, for example, the sentence of Kaehler's student H. E. Weber in *Schriftforschung,* p. 45: "Faith has its Christ, even if science mutilates the Gospels (!) and speaks about the myth of the Son of God in the apostolic proclamation." Kaehler himself, like Bultmann, can write on the basis of 2 Cor. 5:16: "Even if we have known the Messiah according to the flesh, we now, however, know Him no more," or: "The real Christ is the Christ who is preached" (Kaehler, p. 44).

136. Add to this two statements: "Everyone must believe, if only for the reason that it is the Word of God and that he discover inwardly that it is the truth" (Luther). "The inner testimony of the Holy Spirit which, in view of the *theopneustia* ("God-breathed") of Holy Scripture makes the human heart certain and seals it, is the primary and final reason for recognizing the divine origin of Holy Scripture and for believing it with God-given faith" (Hollaz; both statements cited in Hirsch, *Hilfsbuch,* pp. 88 and 377 respectively. [For *theopneustia* see 2 Tim. 3:16; also *Lutheran Cyclopedia,* p. 763.]

137. Cf. the Bankok Documents, in which the concept "festival" displaces the concepts "truth" and "theology," for example in the Letter to the Churches.

138. It is also interesting to note what the philosopher Hans Albert states polemically on the certainty of faith in Ebeling (Albert, pp. 13 ff.).

139. With this result we differ with Hengel, who writes: "The New Testament writings do not require for their interpretation the accession of a supplementary, specific 'theological method of interpretation' which differs qualitatively from all 'historical methods'" (Hengel, p. 89, Thesis 4.3). We

differ also with Stuhlmacher, who claims "the historical-critical method is for us an indispensable working tool for the scholarly investigation of texts—a tool that must constantly be scrutinized as to its capacity to do the job" (p. 19). Cf. also, e. g., Ott, p. 46.

140. Quoted from Hirsch, *Hilfsbuch,* p. 310; similar in Calixt, ibid., p. 311.

141. Italics ours.

142. Cf. Ott, pp. 36 ff.

143. Cf. ibid., pp. 43 f.

144. *Anfaenge der dialektischen Theologie,* I (second ed., 1966), 142 (J. Moltmann, ed.). *Pneuma Christou:* Spirit of Christ.

145. In another sense, however, than was required, for example, in the nominalism of late scholasticism. Cf. Oberman, pp. 54 ff.

146. Because of the great number of possible examples, individual references are utterly impossible.

147. For example, Matt. 9:13; 11:4 ff.; 19:3 ff.; 21:16; 22:23 ff., 41 ff.

148. *Ketubim* ["Writings"]: the third Jewish division of the Old Testament—Job, Psalms, Proverbs, Song of Solomon, Ruth, Lamentations, Ecclesiastes, Esther, Daniel, Ezra, Nehemiah, and Chronicles.

149. Cf. 4 Q flor; 4 Q p Ps. 37.

150. Matt. 12:38 ff. and parallel passages; 16:4.

151. Especially Acts 2:14 ff.

152. Cf., for example, Rom. 9—11 (and my notes in *Mensch und freier Wille,* pp. 366 ff.) or the trend of thought in Gal. 3 and 4.

153. 2 Tim. 3:16; 2 Peter 1:19 ff. [For *theopneustia* see footnote 136.]

154. 1 Cor. 7:40; 2 Cor. 3; 2 Peter 1:16 ff.; John 16:13 ff.; 21:24; 1 John 1:1 ff.; Rev. 1:11.

155. Rev. 22:18 f.

156. Luke 1:1-4.

157. Matt. 1:1; John 1:1.

158. Note the introduction and the concept of the Gospel in relation to Is. 40, especially Is. 40:9.

159. Cf. the *passivum divinum* [divine passive] *dotheisa* [given], v. 15.

160. Cf. also John 2:22: Scripture and the word of Jesus!

161. Cf. as an eminent exposition of the opposing point of view Weber, *Schriftforschung,* pp. 252 ff., especially p. 263: "There are statements in the Bible which immediately demand authority. But it would be foolish to maintain that the Bible contains *only* such statements."

162. Here and for what follows cf. Weber, *Schriftforschung,* pp. 253 ff.

163. The explanations of Oberman, pp. 339 ff., show this. He attempts to correct the previously current viewpoint, such as enunciated in Weber, p. 255.

164. IV Sent d 1 94a3H. The well-known definition of his teaching as "book religion" (Kropatscheck) should better be given up in the light of this and other statements by G. Biel.

165. According to Hirsch, *Hilfsbuch,* p. 94.

166. Taken from *Von Menschenlehre zu meiden,* 1522 (quoted in Hirsch, *Hilfsbuch,* p. 88).

167. Taken from *Assertio omnium articulorum,* 1520 (quoted in Hirsch, *Hilfsbuch,* p. 85).

168. The term "orthodoxy," meaning "true faith," applies in a broader sense to the period of Protestant church history beginning after Luther and ending with the rise of Pietism [in the late 17th century. David Hollaz, 1648—1713, of Pomerania wrote *Examen theologicum acroamaticum,* considered to be the last of the great textbooks of Lutheran orthodoxy.—*Lutheran Cyclopedia,* 1954 ed., p. 479.]

169. Cf. Hirsch, *Hilfsbuch,* pp. 310 f. and 319 respectively.

170. Still quoted in the New Testament! Cf. Heb. 11:37; 2 Peter 1:19; Jude 4, 6, 9, 13 f., etc.

171. Cf. Col. 4:15 f.

172. As an example the insertion of manuscript D after Luke 6:4 is cited. As an example of a traditonal word of Jesus outside of the Gospels, but in the canon, cf. Acts 20:35.

173. Although, for example, Sirach, Tobit, Wisdom of Solomon, and 2 Maccabees are quoted in the New Testament.

174. Hollaz says: "After God willed that what among revealed things is necessary to know for salvation be gathered together in certain books, and since there are no new revelations, the skill of theology is based on those old revelations which were experienced directly by the prophets and apostles and put into writing as the only and adequate principle" (quoted in Hirsch, *Hilfsbuch,* p. 310). We consider inappropriate the pragmatic basis in Ott, pp. 45 f.

175. Cf. Weber, p. 261, with Ott, pp. 45 ff., and Zahrnt, pp. 169 ff.

176. Weber, ibid.

177. Hirsch, *Hilfsbuch,* p. 314. Also Weber, p. 256. Matthias Flacius, born 1520 in Albona, Croatia; died in Frankfurt 1575. [Flacius became famous with his polemical writings against various false teachers in Lutheranism.] He ranks as one of Luther's outstanding students.

178. This was said by Musaeus (quoted in Hirsch, *Hilfsbuch,* p. 314).

179. More details may be found in Weber, pp. 253 ff., and in Hirsch, *Hilfsbuch,* p. 315. Conciliarists: members of a trend in the medieval church that paid more attention to the Bible and to church councils than to the pope.

180. Bengel still speaks of the Biblical authors as "secretaries" and "clerks" *(Kanzellist).* Cf. Maelzer, pp. 362 f. [Johann Albrecht Bengel, 1687—1752, was an outstanding exegete in Wuerttemberg, in southwestern Germany.]

181. For this and for what follows see Hirsch, *Hilfsbuch,* pp. 314 f., and Weber, pp. 256 ff.

182. *Clavis Scripturae Sacrae,* reprint, Frankfurt, 1719, II, 8, 62, 646 f. (quoted in Hirsch, *Hilfsbuch,* p. 314).

183. Weber (p. 261) is critical of this development.

184. About him cf. footnote 180 and Maelzer, pp. 364 f.

185. Gloege, *Kanon*, p. 40; Jesus Christ, of course, is the Logos, the Word.

186. The rebuke of such "fundamentalistic" verbal inspiration found in Ott (p. 46) uses three arguments: (a) historical consciousness, (b) intellectual integrity, and (c) the fact of the Incarnation. Like Maelzer's (p. 368) criticism of Bengel, it suffers from (a) a misconception of the capacity of human consciousness, (b) an equating of integrity with a certain partiality, and (c) a misunderstanding of the Incarnation.

187. Lev. 11:6.

188. Joshua 10:12 ff.

189. It would be well for theology to acknowledge the surmounting of a specific world view *(Weltbild)* by natural science and also to recognize the work of some of its representatives, such as Faraday, P. Jordan, Rohrbach, or Schaaffs.

190. We are reminded of J. A. Bengel's conception of an authentic original text of the Bible.

191. Anthropological: in the sense of a doctrine of man.

192. Joshua 23:14; 1 Kings 8:56.

193. Rengstorf, pp. 415 ff.

194. 2 Sam. 10:1 ff.

195. Cf. Matt. 25:31 ff.; 28:20b; Luke 9:48; John 13:20; 2 Cor. 5:20; Gal. 4:14, and others.

196. There are numerous examples, e. g.: 1 Kings 22; Jer. 8:10 f.; 20:1 ff.; 23:9 ff.; 26:7 ff.; 28:10 f.; Amos 7:10 ff.; Matt. 7:15 ff.; Rom. 16:17 ff.; Phil. 3:2; Col. 2:8 ff.; Rev. 13 and 17.

197. Again, as examples: Gen. 12:10 ff.; 27; Ex. 32; Deut. 32:50 f.; 1 Kings 19; Matt. 20:20 ff.; 26:69 ff.; Acts 6:1 ff.; Gal. 2:11 ff.

198. John 8:46; 2 Cor. 5:21; 1 Peter 2:22; 1 John 3:5; Heb. 4:15.

199. For example, Ps. 137.

200. Cf. Acts 19:21; 23:11; 27:24.

201. Cf. the example in Hirsch, *Hilfsbuch,* p. 86.

202. Since Scripture itself makes use of this; cf. Jesus' use of the Book of Jonah in John 2:18 ff.; Matt. 12:38 ff.; 16:4.

203. Luther, 1539, *Von den Conziliis und Kirchen:* "They (councils) do not teach, but they defend, so that nothing new is preached against the old doctrine" (quoted in Hirsch, *Hilfsbuch,* p. 13).

204. Jer. 31:31 ff.; Matt. 16:18; 18:19 f.; Rev. 1:18; 21:3 ff., and others. For this reason one cannot equate Jewish and Christian tradition because of the concept of tradition and, for example, simply compare the "rules of the elders" with the development of church doctrine.

205. By the way, a legitimate Biblical conviction. Cf. Deut. 18:21 f.

206. 1 Sam. 13:7 ff.

207. 2 Sam. 16:5 ff.

208. Also certain documents of the World Council of Churches.

209. From the standpoint of natural science one may here compare Goedan, pp. 182 ff.

210. For example, in the Theses of July 1530, No. 20 (Hirsch, *Hilfsbuch,* p. 10).

211. "Agreement among the nations"

212. Here one of the pioneers in German theology is still Ethelbert Stauffer, for example, in his book *Christus und die Caesaren,* Hamburg, 1952.

213. St. Paul even quoted from them, as in Titus 1:12 (Epimenides); Acts 17:28 (Aratus, Pseudo-Epimenides); 1 Cor. 15:33 (Menander).

214. Without thereby completely excluding the *possibility* that divine truth may also be found in other religions.

215. Apologetics: the branch of theology which concerns itself with defending the Christian faith. [An "Apology" is work in defense of doctrines that have been attacked, such as the Apology of the Augsburg Confession.]

216. Rom. 1:18 ff.

217. Marxsen, pp. 143 ff. Cf. here, by the way, the warning statements of Stuhlmacher, *Thesen,* pp. 23 ff.

218. Maelzer, pp. 311 ff.

219. Examples from Scripture: Jer. 31:31 ff.; Joel 3; Matt. 5:21-38; 19:3 ff.; 26:28, and parallels; John 1:17; Acts 3:21 ff.; 2 Cor. 3:6 ff.; Rom. 5:20; Gal. 3:19 ff; Heb. 3:1 ff.; 7:11 ff.

220. Which must not be confused with "Law" and "Gospel." Cf. Luther's Preface to the Old Testament, 1523 (quoted in Hirsch, *Hilfsbuch,* pp. 89 ff.).

221. Concerning Calvin see Hirsch, *Hilfsbuch,* pp. 112 ff.

222. Again, see Hirsch, *Hilfsbuch,* pp. 112 ff.

223. Cf. Hirsch, *Hilfsbuch,* p. 92. Luther states concerning the last point: "But what now are the other books of the prophets and the histories? Answer: nothing other than what Moses is." From the Preface to the Old Testament, 1523 (quoted in Hirsch, *Hilfsbuch,* p. 90).

224. Trillhaas, p. 75; *dicta probantia:* prooftexts from Scripture.

225. Heb. 8:5; 9:23; 10:1

226. Col. 2:17 and 1 Cor. 10:11 respectively.

227. Cf. the Pauline logic in Rom. 10:13 ff.

228. *Exkurs:* a special explanation. [This word in the German text has been translated as "a separate little treatise."]

229. Stuhlmacher, *Thesen,* p. 22.

230. Cf. ibid., pp. 21 f.

231. Ibid., p. 23.

232. Cf. 2 Peter 3:15.

233. Rom. 2:4; 2 Peter 3:9, 15; 1 Cor. 13:4 ff.; Rom. 12:20 f.

234. E. g., Matt. 7:13 f.; John 14:6; Acts 4:12; Rom. 3:23 ff.; Rev. 22:14 f.

235. Dualism: the conception, usually religious, according to which there are two dominant opposing forces, such as good and evil, God and Satan.

236. Acts 2:11.

237. Col. 1:16; cf. 1 Cor. 8:6; Heb. 1:2, and others.

238. Here see Ott, p. 46. The Lutheran examples in Hirsch, *Hilfsbuch,* pp. 91 f., are also not worthy of imitation. Similarly Weber, *Schriftforschung,* p. 36.

BIBLIOGRAPHY

With List of Abbreviations Used in the Notes

Albert, H. *Theologische Holzwege.* Tuebingen, 1973.
Abbr.: Albert.

Barth, K. *Gesamtausgabe,* V, *Briefe,* Band 1, Karl Barth—Rudolf Bultmann, *Briefwechsel 1922—1966.* Zuerich, 1971.
Abbr.: Barth.

Bartsch, H.-W., ed. *Kerygma und Mythos,* Band I, 5. Aufl. Hamburg-Bergstedt, 1967.
Abbr.: Bartsch, ed., *Kerygma und Mythos.*

Boehmer, H. *Der Junge Luther,* 5. Aufl. Stuttgart, 1962.
Abbr.: Boehmer, *Luther.*

Boehmer, H. *Luther im Lichte der neueren Forschung,* 4. Aufl. Leipzig und Berlin, 1917.
Abbr.: Boehmer, *Forschung.*

Bornkamm, H., ed. *Martin Luthers Vorreden zur Bibel.* Hamburg, 1967.
Abbr.: Bornkamm.

Bultmann, R. *Die Geschichte der synoptischen Tradition,* 6. Aufl. Goettingen, 1964.
Abbr.: Bultmann, *Tradition.*

Bultmann, R. *Theologie des Neuen Testaments,* 5. Aufl. Tuebingen, 1965.
Abbr.: Bultmann, *Theologie.*

Falckenberg, R. *Geschichte der neueren Philosophie,* 8. Aufl. Berlin und Leipzig, 1921.
Abbr.: Falckenberg.

Feghelm, H. *Um die rechte Auslegung der Bibel,* Liebenzeller Studienhefte, 4. Bad Liebenzell, 1967.
Abbr.: Feghelm.

Goedan, H. *Die Unzustaendigkeit der Seele.* Stuttgart, 1961.
Abbr.: Goedan.

Hahn, F. "Probleme historischer Kritik," *Zeitschrift fuer die neutestamentliche Wissenschaft und die Kunde des Urchristentums,* 63 (1972), 1—17.
Abbr.: Hahn.

Hengel, M. "Historische Methoden und theologische Auslegung des Neuen Testaments," *Kerygma und Dogma,* 2 (1973), 85—90.
Abbr.: Hengel.

Hirsch, E. *Hilfsbuch zum Studium der Dogmatik,* 4. Aufl. Berlin, 1964.
Abbr.: Hirsch, *Hilfsbuch.*

Joest, W. "Ueberlegungen zu Thema Theologie und Wissenschaft," *Kerygma und Dogma,* 2 (1973), 150—56.
Abbr.: Joest.

Kaehler, M. *Der sogenannte historische Jesus und der geschichtliche, biblische Christus,* neu hrsg. von E. Wolf, 3. Aufl. Muenchen, 1961.
Abbr.: Kaehler.

Kaesemann, E., ed. *Das Neue Testament als Kanon.* Goettingen, 1970.
Abbr.: *Kanon.*

Kaesemann, E. *Exegetische Versuche und Besinnungen,* 1. und 2. Band. Goettingen, 1964.
Abbr.: Kaesemann, I; Kaesemann, II.

Kuemmel, W. G. *Das Neue Testament, Geschichte der Erforschung seiner Probleme,* 2. Aufl. Freiburg und Muenchen, 1970.
Abbr.: Kuemmel.

Lessing, G. E. *Die Erziehung des Menschengeschlechts und andere Schriften,* Reclam Books, No. 8968.
Abbr.: Lessing.

Maier, G. "Mensch und freier Wille nach den juedischen Religionsparteien zwischen Ben Sira und Paulus," *Wissenschaftliche Untersuchungen zum Neuen Testament,* 12. Tuebingen, 1971.
Abbr.: *Mensch und freier Wille.*

Maelzer, G. *Johann Albrecht Bengel.* Stuttgart, 1970.
Abbr.: Maelzer.

Marxsen, W. *Einleitung in das Neue Testament,* 2. Aufl. Guetersloh, 1964.
Abbr.: Marxsen.

Oberman, H. A. *Spaetscholastik und Reformation,* Band I. Zuerich, 1965.
Abbr.: Oberman.

Ott, H. *Die Antwort des Glaubens,* 1. Aufl. Stuttgart und Berlin, 1972.
Abbr.: Ott.

Pascal, B. *Gedanken.* Reclam Books, No. 1621/22.
Abbr.: Pascal.

Rengstorf, K. H. The article "Apostello" etc., in *Theologisches Woerterbuch zum Neuen Testament,* I (Stuttgart, 1933), 397—448.
Abbr.: Rengstorf.

Semler, J. S. "Abhandlung von freier Untersuchung des Canon," *Texte zur Kirchen- und Theologiegeschichte,* 5. Guetersloh, 1967.
Abbr.: Semler.

Stuhlmacher, P. "Neues Testament und Hermeneutik-Versuch einer Bestandsaufnahme," *Zeitschrift fuer Theologie und Kirche,* 68 (1971), 121—61.
Abbr.: Stuhlmacher, *Hermeneutik.*

Stuhlmacher, P. "Thesen zur Methodologie gegenwaertiger Exegese," *Zeitschrift*

fuer die neutestamentliche Wissenschaft und die Kunde des Urchristentums, 63 (1972), 18—26.
Abbr.: Stuhlmacher, *Thesen.*

Trillhaas, W. *Dogmatik.* Berlin, 1962.
Abbr.: Trillhaas.

Troeltsch, E. "Die wissenschaftliche Lage und ihre Anforderungen an die Theologie," *Sammlung gemeinverstaendlicher Vortraege und Schriften aus dem Gebiet der Theologie und Religionsgeschichte,* 20. Tuebingen, 1900.
Abbr.: Troeltsch, *Lage.*

Troeltsch, E. "Ueber historische und dogmatische Methode in der Theologie," *Gesammelte Schriften,* Zweiter Band, Neudruck der 2. Aufl. (1922). Aalen, 1962, pp. 729—53.
Abbr.: Troeltsch, *Methode.*

Weber, H. E. *Historisch-kritische Schriftforschung und Bibelglaube,* 2. Aufl. Guetersloh, 1914.
Abbr.: Weber, *Schriftforschung.*

Weber, O. *Grundlage der Dogmatik,* Band 1. Neukirchen/Moers, 1959.
Abbr.: Weber.

Zahrnt, H. *Gott kann nicht sterben.* Muenchen, 1970.
Abbr.: Zahrnt.

GLOSSARY

*Words and expressions identified with an asterisk have been added to the author's list in their entirety, or his definitions were expanded by the translator.

Analog—noun.
Anything analogous to something else.

*Analogous—adjective.
Resembling in certain respects.

*Analogy—noun.
Resemblance of properties or relations; similarity without identity. Reasoning in which from certain observed and known relations or parallel resemblances others can be inferred. A comparison or correspondence between two things.

*Canon—noun.
A word derived from the Greek which means "rule." The adjective "canonical" means something has been accepted as the rule. Over the centuries the adjective has come to mean "divine" or "inspired" when applied to the 39 books of the Old Testament and the 27 books of the New Testament. These 66 "divinely inspired" books of the Bible are "the canon."

*Canon in the Canon—idiom.
An expression of higher criticism which implies that certain portions of the canon are *not* recognized as God's Word in the same measure as other portions. Higher critics have therefore sought out those portions of Scripture which have "most validity" and have referred to these as the "canon in the canon."

*Content Criticism—idiom.
Name given to the type of higher criticism which evaluates a given

Biblical book on the basis of what the critic believes *should have been* written. German theologians use the term *Sachkritik*.

*Documentary Hypothesis—idiom.

During the latter half of the 19th century higher criticism rejected the Mosaic authorship of the Pentateuch, maintaining that at least portions of the five books of Moses are based on four other sources, written between 950 B.C. and 450 B. C. These other sources, or *documents*, they identified respectively as J, E, D, and P. This theory, that books of the Bible were written by authors other than those usually identified as the authors, or at least portions were written by other authors, was later applied to most Old Testament books and some New Testament books.

Dogmatics—noun.

The branch of theology which concerns itself with church doctrine— arranging, teaching, and defending it.

*Eschatology—noun.

The part of dogmatics or doctrinal theology that treats of last things— immortality, the resurrection, life after death, the second coming of Christ, the final judgment, and the end of the world. Adjective: eschatological.

Exegesis—noun.

The branch of theology that, literally, "leads out" or "leads forth" from the original Bible language the real meaning of a Scripture text or portion of Scripture. Interpretation. The theologian engaged in this work is known as an *exegete*.

*Form Criticism—idiom.

Term applied to an early 20th century development in higher criticism as a reaction to radical Biblical criticism. Its first exponent, Hermann Gunkel, believed that much of Scripture was *orally* transmitted before it was actually written. Gunkel therefore speculated on how the written text developed into the *form* it has today. By 1919 such leading German theologians as Dibelius, Schmidt, and Bultmann applied this theory to the Gospels (cf. footnote 76).

*Historiographer—noun.

Usually a historian who has been designated to write official history; one who is acquainted with the principles of historical research and with methods of recording history.

*Inspiration—noun.

The doctrine which holds that the Holy Spirit exercised a special influence on human beings who wrote the books of the Bible. The result was that what they wrote was the Word of God. *Verbal inspiration* holds that the Holy Spirit "inspired" the holy writers to write the exact individual words (in the original languages) He wanted them to write.

*Methodology—noun.
"That section of the preliminary work in the general study of theology which pertains to the form of study and the methods of attacking the problem of study" *(Lutheran Cyclopedia,* 1954 edition, p. 674).

*Norm—noun.
A standard, especially one accepted as an authority.

Normative—adjective.
Meeting the requirements of a standard.

*Redaction Criticism—idiom.
Term applied to the most recent development in higher criticism, which is a reaction against *form criticism.* This theory holds that the writers of the Gospels were not historians, but theologians. To develop their own respective theologies, they ascribed to Jesus words He never spoke and they credit Him with things He never did. These "inventions" were necessary, according to this theory, in order to have a basis for the theology the writers wanted to develop.

Revelation—noun.
As used in this book (spelled with a lower-case letter), this word refers to everything God has revealed to man in His Word. The Biblical book Revelation (of St. John the Divine) is capitalized.

Structure—noun.
The manner in which a portion of Scripture is constructed and arranged.

*Systematics—noun.
"The branch of theology that tries to express all religious truth in self-consistent statements forming an organized whole" *(Lutheran Cyclopedia,* p. 750).

*Variant—noun.
Differing forms of the same word, such as different spellings, or different endings, often considered to be copyists' errors in old Biblical manuscripts. "Smith," "Smyth," "Smythe," and "Smitty" are all *variants* of a common English name.